I0058112

# THE DEVELOPMENT ALTERNATIVE
Powerful Strategies for Unparalleled Business Results

Sophia Sanchez

Develop For Results International Publishing

Tampa, Florida USA

Copyright © 2014 by **Sophia Sanchez**

All rights reserved. No part of this publication may be reproduced, distributed or transmitted in any form or by any means, without prior written permission.

**Develop For Results International Publishing**
**www.DevelopForResults.com**

Publisher's Note: The Author has strived in every way to be as accurate and complete as possible in the creation of this book, notwithstanding the fact that she does not warrant or represent at any time that the contents within the book will remain the same due to the rapidly changing nature of the subject. While all attempts have been made to verify every piece of information provided in this publication, the Author assumes no responsibility for omissions, or contrary interpretation of the subject matter herein.

**The Development Alternative / Sophia Sanchez**

This book is dedicated to all those who have a passion for developing others and take action to do so within their organizations, whether they are in a leadership position or not.
Current and aspiring business leaders, this book is dedicated to you and to your success!

# Contents

# PROLOGUE

In the year 2001, I started my career in Human Resources.

I decided to enter the profession in pursuit of my passion for coaching and developing people, which I have learned to value from being in different leadership roles since the early stages of my working ventures. I learned at a very young age that educating, coaching, and holding my subordinates accountable for their fates in the job they are doing, makes succeeding in my position a lot easier.

Through my various leadership roles, I have purposely chosen to take the stand of coaching others on the best ways to resolve their own problems, versus giving them the solutions. Which really is one of the best, if not the only way, to encourage and foster development.

With that mindset and extraordinary results from my coaching engagements, I decided that HR would be a perfect career for me to end up in. Soon after completing my Masters, I was recruited and fortunate enough to contribute to various organizations, on both national and international assignments. Capitalizing on my expertise in the areas of coaching, development, and employee engagement, I have been able to enlighten many executives on the true value of developing their people. To my dismay, and, sad to say, I have also come to realize, that this is not a common practice among Human Resources professionals, neither do executives empower them to bring out such value to the organizations they support. While the HR profession has come a long way in positioning itself and claiming its role as a partner in meeting business objectives, I believe it is important that I point out that there is still a lot of improvement needed in the field before HR professionals can live up to that title.

Hence, I urge every leader, and executive, accountable for business results to take the lead in implementing a culture of learning and development within their organizations. Unless your HR people play a vital role in planning your business objectives, and are accountable for results, I advise against entrusting them with championing your organizational development strategies, as those strategies will only be successful when carefully aligned with the business objectives they support.

# CHAPTER ONE

# INTRODUCTION

**When it comes to running a successful business, what do you think is most critical to your company's bottom line?**

I asked this question of some of the business leaders I have consulted with. Some feel that having a strong product line and loyal client base is crucial; strong leadership, and stakeholder involvement were also cited. While these avenues do provide their business with much-needed direction, very few of these leaders mentioned or understood the true value of their human capital.

If you, of course, mentioned any of the above, you're certainly on the right track. But if you *really* want to reveal the goldmine within your company, the kind that helps increase productivity, improve product processes, and even skyrocket customer-acquisition rates—it's time to consider your employees to be the most important business resource you'll ever have.

And it stands to reason that if you're not using your employees properly, that is, developing them to become productive and prosperous members of the workplace, then your business will eventually hit a wall that it just can't get around.

No matter from which angle you approach it, employee development will play a fundamental role in the success— or demise—of your business efforts. On the one hand, if you give your employees the tools, resources, encouragement, and feedback they need to become better team members, you're essentially setting up your business with a roadmap that outlines precisely how to get to your ultimate goals. On the other hand, if you treat your employees as the proverbial "cogs in the machine," you're denying your organization one of the most critical components of financial success.

Regardless what your organizational goals might be—or how long you've been in business—it pays to carefully analyze how your company approaches employee development. Yes, it starts with the executive, leader, accountable business partner to set the tone for that development culture to blossom.

Before we get to the details of how you can implement development programs within your organization, it's important to answer one of the most basic questions that organizational leaders *and* business owners have when they approach this book:

Just *why* are productive, creative, and successful employees so fundamental to a company's success?

Let's answer this question from a multi-faceted point of view.

## The Research

There's a wealth of research that supports the notion that employee development can be critical to the success of an organization, no matter what its strategic and operational goals are. For example, the University of Minnesota argues that a review of research literature in 2003 supported the commonly-held belief that employee-development programs make positive and lasting contributions to overall performance levels within the organization. A more highly-skilled workforce can accomplish more as the individuals gain in experience and knowledge. What's more, retaining a happy employee that you've invested in saves your company a great deal of money. One such method of retention is to provide opportunities for your employees to develop new skills. In research conducted to assess what retained employees, development was one of the top three retention items.[1]

Another interesting piece of research asserts that in order to create motivated and productive employees, it's not enough to find "self-starters" or "persistent" candidates for available job roles; after all, even the most

---

[1] http://www1.umn.edu/ohr/toolkit/development/

determined go-getter can lose steam in an unsupportive and draining work environment. In a white paper published by The Ken Blanchard Companies, the following items were listed as most important for creating motivated and happy employees:[2]

- Meaningful work
- Autonomy
- Task Variety
- Workload Balance
- Feedback

This white paper asserts that sometimes it's not as simple as managing employees; in fact, one could even argue that *too much* supervision could actually harm any efforts to produce highly-motivated employees who are thrilled to work at your company.

In another interesting research revelation, the latest State of the American Workplace report demonstrated that almost 70 percent of U.S. workers don't like their jobs.[3] This contributes to an environment where employees are not only disinterested in their jobs; they have no desire to be productive, motivated, and enthusiastic in the workplace. One doesn't have to be a rocket scientist to understand that the more disinterested and lackadaisical employees within an organization, the more likely it is that

---

[2] http://www.kenblanchard.com/Leading-Research/Research/Employee-Work-Passion-Volume-4

[3] http://www.gallup.com/strategicconsulting/163007/state-american-workplace.aspx

the business will suffer in terms of productivity, and eventually, the bottom line.

This research might paint a doom-and-gloom portrait for companies that haven't already embraced employee development. Fortunately, your organization can still enjoy the benefits of such programs, no matter when you roll out the changes (although it stands to reason that sooner is most definitely better). Multiple case studies and publications have shown that companies can experience a significant shift for the better, thanks to an investment in employee development. Below are some examples:

- Employee Development is about ensuring that workers feel connected to something bigger than themselves, both socially and intellectually. Research shows that in much of the global workplace, simple connections and involvement meet the more altruistic and basic human needs of feeling connected and being part of something greater than themselves.[4]

- Employee development centers on creating a culture that's productive and geared towards workers. For example, Google is renowned for having the kind of environment that employees want to work in. From gourmet kitchens stacked with free food to on-site laundry service, Google gets that employees are the lifeblood of the organization—and it seeks to reward

---

[4] http://www.forbes.com/sites/sylviavorhausersmith/2013/08/14/how-the-best-places-to-work-are-nailing-employee-engagement/

workers in ways that aren't always linked to financial compensation (although that certainly can help)[5]

- Employee development is about acknowledging contributions to the company, no matter how large or small they might be. For example, DHL Express has established a significant track record of thanking employees for engagement within the organization. While financial compensation is often used to thank employees, DHL Express often uses honorary ceremonies, black-tie events, and even notes of appreciation to show that they care. Research suggests that they're on the right track. Employees who are rewarded in non-compensatory ways (for example, with awards, changes in titles, more meaningful work, etc.) are more likely to be satisfied and enthusiastic within the workplace than employees who are given financial rewards (such as raises and bonuses).

While these may just be a few compelling examples from thousands of demonstrations of employee development, the point is clear: the more an organization invests in an employee, the more likely that employee is going to be more productive, satisfied, loyal, and invested in the overall success of the business. When employees are invested in the organization, the business really achieves.

With that in mind, it's important to look at why some organizations may not already be investing in

---

[5]http://books.google.com/books/about/Case_study_Corporate_culture.html?id=LYU2hwgcrUsC

employee development, despite hundreds upon thousands of case studies that extol the benefits of happy and motivated employees.

## Why Aren't More Companies Investing in Employees?

Ask any Human Resources professional or Business Leader how important employees are to an organization's overall success, and it's likely that they'll give an overwhelmingly positive answer. But, like the old saying goes, there's a difference between "talk the talk" and "walk the walk"—unless a company is truly committed to a culture of learning and development, they're just spouting off a tired speaking point.

Company leadership often understands that employees are important—however that doesn't always mean they're ready to make the financial and emotional commitment to providing employees with the tools and resources they need to become more productive. These are the same company leaders who know that losing an employee can cost more than retaining one (in fact, businesses in the United States lose over $10 billion a year to employee turnover.) But what these leaders might not realize is that disengaged employees—that is, the workers who aren't as productive and motivated as they could be—cost the American workplace an astonishing *$450 to $550 billion every year.*

That astonishing figure comes from the fact that employees who are disengaged in the workplace are far more likely to make costly mistakes, require more supervision, and cost more in general to maintain. What's more, these employees aren't motivated by more flex time or paid vacation days. They're suffering from what I like to call a "sense of purposelessness"—for them to become more engaged, motivated, and happy in the workplace, they need to connect with a viable and meaningful purpose.

Business owners and executives who convince themselves that they don't have the monetary means to invest in employee development are actually losing far more money than they would ever spend on development programs in the first place. However, many times, a lack of employee development within the workplace happens for the following reasons:

- There's a lack of clear goals, directions, and priorities. Remember, motivated and productive employees need to feel a real sense of connection with a bigger purpose. That means outlining organizational goals and mission to employees, and connecting them with reasons as to why they are fundamental to achieving these goals. They can't be cliché reasons, either—employees need to see and *feel* that their work makes a real difference. They also need to be held accountable for meeting those goals that are directly related to your business needs.

- There's a clear lack of role definition within the workplace. Employees need to firmly understand what they are contributing in the workplace. Progress and productivity can be hard to achieve if your employees don't understand how they are helping a project or the organization in general. This may not only affect the employee, but a lack of clearly-defined roles can also cause tension between other employees. Think about it this way: if there's too much overlap between your employees, they could end up doubling up on work, which is a waste of their talents, and the organization's time and resources—a trend that I have observed in organizations, especially when there is a lack of communication and definition of purpose.

- There's a lack of cooperation and trust in the workplace. Motivated and productive employees need to feel support from leadership, e.g. their immediate supervisors, and the Human Resource professionals that support them. If the workplace environment operates based on a lack of trust and cooperation (for example, if employees feel micromanaged, or inefficient leaders are promoted), employees are more likely to feel dissatisfied and disinterested in the company's success.

- There's a lack of engagement from "higher-ups," including managers, executive-level members, and even Human-Resources professionals. As previously mentioned, your employees want to know that they're making a real and significant contribution to the workplace. If a company's executives hardly interact with employees (or worse, they don't interact at all), there's only so much your employees can do before they feel that a traditional corporate hierarchy is holding them back.

Take a look at all the reasons why employee development might not be implemented within the workplace and carefully scour through the reasons. Notice that none of them have anything to do with significant financial investments and other monetary costs? That's right! Many organizational leaders believe that to implement employee-development programs in the workplace would require a substantial investment in time and money, but it can often be solved with clear communication, more trust, cooperation, and the willingness to let your employees take creative risks.

That's precisely where this book comes into play.

## How to Use This Book

This employee-development guide will focus on critical aspects of worker development designed for business leaders responsible for bottom-line business objectives. The overall goal is to help these organizational leaders get the results they want from their most valuable business asset:

Their employees.

For Human Resource professionals, this will involve partnering with upper management to align and communicate organizational goals in a way that encourages trust, cooperation, and eventually, employee investment. This means understanding the nature of the business you are supporting, striving to understand the competitors, and building a competitive advantage. Until you can claim your seat at the business decision-making table, as a true partner with the CEOs and executives you support, you will never be successful at aligning business objectives with development, which is the foundation of every development program.

No matter where your organization might be in the process of investing in employee development (or if it hasn't even started at all), this book can provide you with the blueprint necessary for engaging and motivating your employees with meaningful and purposeful work, goals, and strategies.

If you have any questions while reading this book, please don't hesitate to contact me at Sophia.sanchez@DevelopForResults.com. I'd love to hear what you think about these strategies, and how they've worked out in your own organization.

# CHAPTER TWO

# DEVELOPING AND INTRODUCING THE DEVELOPMENT PROGRAM

In the Introduction of this book, we discussed just a few of the many reasons why employee development plays such a critical role in the success of an organization. After all, employee development is all about producing effective, persistent, and enthusiastic workers who are loyal and committed to the business. Development can also significantly strengthen a person's ability to deliver an exceptional product or service to a customer. In that respect, employee development becomes much more than improving morale in the office; it's about ensuring that every aspect of your organization is aligned with your business objectives and committed to delivering the best possible experience for your customers and clients. What's more, employee development can greatly enhance the likelihood that your employees will stay in your company, thus reducing the amount of time and resources you'd have to spend in finding, recruiting, and training new talent.

With that in mind, why don't more organizations invest in employee development?

"I don't want my talent to pursue better positions elsewhere."

It's a base fear that many executives are hesitant to admit, but it's a powerful motivator for why many organizations don't invest as much as they should in their employees. Now, many of these executives have every right in the world to be concerned that their talent will leave; a recent trend indicated that young high achievers are more likely to leave a company after just twenty-eight months. This is especially relevant in our own day and age, where top talent is younger, hungrier, and less committed to the "antiquated" idea of employee loyalty. Previous generations were much more comfortable with the idea of spending decades in the same business; whereas workers today may work at fifteen different companies before they're ready for retirement. This represents a significant change from yesteryears, when men and women born between 1957 and 1964 held an average of 11 jobs throughout the duration of their careers. With that in mind, it's important to acknowledge the common executive fear that employees will take all that training and bring it to another company.

However, as I often point out to the executives, and managers with whom I partner, withholding training and coaching isn't exactly the most productive response to these fears. In fact, it makes it much more likely that employees will take their talents elsewhere, as they may not feel like they're being supported by their leadership (and rightly so). Employees need to feel as though their leadership is investing in their success. Think of it this way:

if you invest in the success of your employees, some will eventually move on, but others will stay; what's more, the company's reputation as an excellent employer will make recruitment easier, as you'll be able to attract top talent in droves.

When executives and human-resource professionals work together to form an employee-development program, great things happen. Employees are more satisfied and engaged at work (thus helping you avoid becoming a part of that dreaded $450-550 billion in lost dollars from disengaged employees). Employees are more likely to stay at your company longer, which means that you will experience more benefits from top-tier talent. After all, employees know when they're working for a company that excels in employee retention. No business in any industry treats employees the same; therefore, if employees feel happy and valued at your organization, they'll be less likely to search for greener pastures.

What's more, the company's reputation can help attract new talent as well as enhance relationships with customers. In today's engaged and socially-conscious world, customers *want* to spend their money at organizations that are conscientious and kind to their employees. Consider the success stories that are illustrated by companies like Whole Foods, which pays full-time employees health benefits, and Starbucks, which actively recruits veterans to work for their brand. The more customers hear about companies that are truly committed to employee success, the more likely they are to take their hard-earned dollars to those organizations. Word gets around quickly on how a business treats its employees—and customers are all too happy to voice their opinions with their dollars.

Employee development also makes it possible for workers to feel better about taking creative and strategic risks. When an organization demonstrates that it values its employees as people (and not just as an asset), it gives employees the courage and confidence they need to take the kind of risks that may result in significant payoffs. Consider this: if you're an employee working for a company with high employee turnover and little-to-no support from leadership, chances are very slim that you'll feel compelled to take a creative risk with a product or process. In fact, you're much more likely to keep your proverbial nose to the grindstone for fear of making waves and losing your job.

On the other hand, consider being an employee in a company that's genuinely committed to the success of its workforce. You regularly interact with your managers and even executive leadership. Your manager provides ongoing coaching, which keeps you informed on his or her expectations, and encourages you to feel more motivated and driven in your current position. You're empowered to take risks in the workplace—and you're not afraid to approach your leadership with new and exciting changes to a standard product process. Regardless of whether that idea works out or not, you don't worry about being reprimanded or having your idea fall on deaf ears; in fact, you're rewarded for your risk-taking efforts.

The latter example is precisely the kind of organization that talented employees want to find themselves in—and the kind of workplace that can only be formed by a solid commitment to employee development.

## Four Traits of a Successful Employee-Development Program

While industries vary across the board, it's fortunate that employee development programs usually exhibit common characteristics. This can help executive leaders and business professionals better understand what a successful employee-development program looks like—and how to measure it's progress. With this in mind, let's take a look at the common traits of an employee-development program that's destined for business success:

## Trait#1 - The program must be aligned with business objectives.

When your employees want to start contributing to the organization, it's imperative that the employee-development program be as efficient as possible. One way to ensure such efficiency is to directly align their development goals with your business objectives. One business executive with whom I consulted once told me that he was having a hard time explaining to his customer-service team why they could not participate in his division's bonus program. When I asked him why he believes they didn't qualify to participate in the bonus program, he told me "all they do is answer the phone." There was no alignment on how answering and catering to customer needs contribute to meeting business objectives. So, yes, unless those are aligned, and their positions justified to what value they bring, giving them a bonus cannot be justified, which in essence is a lack of preparation from the management and leadership team.

## Trait #2 - The program must place employees in charge.

In charge of their own development, that is. Think about the role that a coach plays in the life of an athlete, an actor, or even an executive professional. It stands to reason that if your employee-development program approaches training and mentoring from the above mentioned perspectives, you'll be much more likely to produce highly motivated, engaged, and enthusiastic employees.

This will not be successful by conducting massive seminars to "train" your employees. It goes back to my initial stand for organizational leaders to foster a culture of development and empowerment. Think of the last time you attended a lecture that droned on and on. Did you leave the lecture feeling fired up? Or did you feel like you stopped paying attention after the first hour slowly ticked by? When employees are lectured—rather than involving them in the development process—that is much more likely to create disinterested, disengaged colleagues. Employees are adults that are more than capable of learning how to become stellar players in the workplace. That's why employee-development should focus on providing employees with the resources they need for enhancing their strengths.

What's more, don't limit these resources to what's required for their current role. It may seem counterintuitive to train them for roles and positions that are well beyond what they need to know now, but making the investment now ensures that your employees feel valued. They're more likely to leverage this information into managerial roles within your company. Employees who feel as though they're stuck in their current positions without the proverbial light at the end of the tunnel are more likely to look for better positions in different companies. Offering them the ability to move onward and upward within your company negates the likelihood that this will happen. I'll discuss strategies that can help your employee-development program effectively achieve these traits throughout the course of this book.

## Trait #3 - The program must underscore employee strength.

One of the biggest mistakes I have observed in employee-development programs is when managers invest all their efforts highlighting something that an employee needs to improve. While the intention behind this mistake is certainly a good one, it only serves to subtly berate the employee for not living up to executive expectations. In order for an employee to perform a task, the willingness, skills, and ability have to be present. Hence, the importance of a good selection system, strengths and skills evaluation should have been assessed during the selection process. The employee was hired for a reason—hopefully their skill set for that particular job. Use that as leverage for the business results you need.

## Trait #4 - The program must be championed by the leadership team.

As many of you may agree, certain processes are a no-brainer to organizations, especially those required by law, or adapted as an ethical "must-do," "just because." I am here to tell you that payroll processing can fall into that category; employee development can't. In order for this process to be effective, it has to be championed, or, at the very least, be supported by and be held accountable for by senior leaders. By Senior Leaders I am not referring to your manager or director of Human Resources, especially, if that particular director has no clue which direction the business leaders want the company to go, and nor do they contribute to that vision.

Before you begin investing your company's time, resources, and tools into an employee-development program, carefully assess how your organization stands up to the above criteria. Are you able to provide your employees with the opportunities they need to feel fulfilled, happy, and satisfied that they're making an impact? Are you giving employees the ability to make valuable contributions within your company? Is your disciplinary policy working against you? Does your organization adhere to traditional hierarchal structures, or can your employees access top-tier managers and even executives? Does the program support the company's vision?

By looking at your company within this framework, you can begin to understand how much work needs to be done before rolling out a new employee-development program.

## Six benefits of aligning company objectives with employee - development programs

Employee development represents an ideal opportunity for employers and HR professionals to highlight their company's objectives, missions, and strategic goals. A company's objectives are like a roadmap that provides employees and leadership with the directions they need. In other words, the organization's objectives can help shape how projects should be approached, how many customers a company needs, what the customer service should be like, and what criteria determine the company's success. That means that your company objectives should play a critical role in your employee-development program, as it can help your employees understand how to channel their enthusiasm and motivation. For example, if your company objective is to become a top leader within your respective industry, your employees will understand that taking new and creative risks with products will be encouraged, as it may likely lead to groundbreaking new discoveries.

This is precisely why it's critical for executives, managers, and HR professionals to be in alignment with company objectives. There are many other reasons why aligning company objectives can help enhance your employee-development program, including the following:

- It helps improve success rates for your employee-development program. Sharing company objectives enables employees to understand what minimum performance looks like, and how much of a difference maximum performance can make.

- Both the company and employees save considerable time and effort. In an ideal world, your organization would have unlimited resources; however, that's not always the case. That means it's important to outline your company's objectives, break down the goals from regional, departmental, and all the way down to the individual levels so that your employees understand how their productivity and work should be directed. That means your employees won't have to deal with the frustrating task of re-doing work, which can waste time as well as undermine employee achievement.

- Stakeholder's satisfaction. Your C-level executives, Board of Directors, and other stakeholders want to know that your employees are working towards a singular mission—and incorporating the company mission into your employee-development program can help satisfy that curiosity. What's more, it ensures that everyone is on the same page, which helps make a company run like a well-oiled engine.

- Smarter investments. There's no denying that employee development might seem like an expense at first—and if handled inappropriately, it can be. However, it's the kind of long-term investment that can reap significant rewards later down the line.

- Preserving customer's requirements. At the end of the day, your company's missions and objectives are about providing the best customer experience possible. That's why it's critical to provide your employees with company objectives, as they can help highlight how the products and services make a difference in the lives of customers.

- Promotes success. Whether your employees work within a product process or provide a service directly to customers, incorporating your company's missions within the development program makes it less likely that your employees will fall off track. When your employees understand exactly why a product or service is being provided—and *how* it should be provided—your employees can utilize their productivity and motivation to ensure that success rates are greatly increased.

## How to Define Your Company's Purpose

In order to effectively communicate with your employees during the rollout of the development program, it's important to help them understand what your company is here to do. Employees who don't understand the purpose of your company—as well as how your products or services make an impact in the lives of your customers—may find it difficult to become enthusiastic and motivated, as they won't have a clear definition for what your company does, and nor will they understand its place within your particular industry. This is why it's important to define your mission statement, strategic goals, and other objectives that employees *need* to know and understand.

Whether you're an Operations Manager, business leader, or Human Resources professional, one of your primary roles is to anticipate and communicate organizational goals and objectives with your employees at all times. This is especially relevant in a fast-paced industry, as you can't afford to have employees confused about the purpose of the company and how it impacts customers. Before you communicate your company's purpose with employees, take the following steps to ensure you're developing a clear definition:

- Carefully analyze your company's biggest goals to determine what your mission statement or objectives should be. For example, if your organization already has a mission statement that emphasizes how important customer service is, then you know that you should coach employees to deliver five-star customer service at all times. This might feel like you're working "backwards," but it can usually help you to identify what skills and knowledge need to be imparted to your employees.

- Assess who your customers are, and how the product or service makes a difference in their lives. For example, if your company sells a mobility device that's used by people who have foot injuries, you may want to tell employees how these customers are able to move around better, how they're better able to minimize their injuries, and other benefits. Providing your employees with better coaching ensures that customers are always in the forefront of their minds. What's more, employees who have a connection with customers and feel like they're making a difference are much more likely to be motivated and enthusiastic about their work. After all, employees who feel like they're making meaningful contributions to the world are much more likely to be loyal and productive within the workplace.

- Have a clear idea of which members make up your company's leadership. This may include stakeholders, your Board of Directors, C-level executives, and even investors. This is important to learn about before rolling out your employee-development program, as you want to ensure that your company's leadership is supportive and encouraging of your employees. Remember, employees who work in companies where leadership is intangible or removed from the workplace, are likely to feel insignificant to their employers.

This doesn't involve taking complicated steps to define your company's mission; what's more, it doesn't boil down to understanding industry numbers or how much your company takes in each quarter. These are pieces of quantitative information that may provide meaning for stakeholders and investors, but they're not exactly going to get your employees pumped up and excited. Instead, business leaders and Human Resources personnel need to focus on *qualitative* information; that is, the benefits and reasons that employees need to feel as though their work truly matters within the workplace, the industry, and even the local community.

It's also important for executives to realize that employee-development must be centered on the company's core values; in other words, those values that might not be explicitly stated on the company's mission, but are implicit in the way you conduct and do business. You may label these as ethics or morality, but either way, helping your employees understand what the company values are can go a long way in improving the impact of an employee-development program.

Determining your company values might involve sitting back and seeing what's emphasized in meetings with leadership. For example, do your stakeholders seem to emphasize profits over product quality or delivery? Is business leadership more focused on profit margins? Do business leaders make themselves available to employees for mentoring or have an open door office policy? The more you sit back and observe, the more likely it is that you'll better understand the values of your company.

Ultimately, ensure that any company values and objectives you're communicating really resonate with you. The truth of the matter is that if it doesn't matter to you, it's not going to matter to your employees. Be honest about what matters to you in terms of your company's success. If you want your business to be the top profit earner in your industry, then communicate that to your employees. If you want to build the best reputation for customer service in the area, get excited about it before communicating it to your employees. They're looking to you as an example— and if you're not excited about your company's core objectives, values, and purpose, then they're not going to be, either.

## *Communicating Company Values*

Once you've defined and connected with your company's values, you'll need to communicate these values in a way that will get your employees excited about what your company does. While there's no one-size-fits-all approach to this, it's important to acknowledge that this isn't going to be a one-time episode. Ensuring that your employees are motivated involves continually keeping them in touch with the values of the company. Multiple studies have shown that employees often become unproductive and unmotivated when they feel disconnected from the organization; one of the best ways to keep them excited about the work you do is to continually highlight why *your* business is the best one to work for.

Unfortunately, many business leaders and HR professionals fail to communicate company values in a way that's engaging and exciting. They'll often approach it much like a professor would in a 101 class for freshmen: they'll place the mission statement on a piece of paper or in the employee manual, pass it around and leave it at that. Company values, on the other hand, are a real and fluid thing that needs to be addressed in a way that acknowledges their importance. The bottom line is that you can't expect your employees to be excited about your company's mission and values if you treat them in an unexciting and dismissive manner.

With that in mind, show your employees why your company truly matters. Whenever a customer approaches you with a story as to how your product or service made his or her life better, don't keep it to yourself; instead, let your employees know during a project or team meeting. If there's a major topic trending in your industry, talk with your employees about it and how your company feels regarding this topic. If your company has a particular issue it needs to work out, don't limit brainstorming to your upper management; ask your employees for their opinions and invite them to be creative with their solutions. These are just a few suggestions, but they can really help your employees internalize your company's core values and objectives.

Make sure that you're communicating with your employees in a way that's productive, inclusive, and clear. Don't limit discussion about your company's values to a quarterly or annual meeting; bring them up in department meetings, or even in informal coaching sessions. Don't discuss them in a dry and formal way, as this may make your employees feel as though you're reading from a script. Approach communicating your company values as you would your personal values. For example, if you want your company to be creative leaders in your industry, encourage your employees to regularly brainstorm and take creative risks. This helps to make your company values a real and tangible thing, rather than just words tucked away in an employee handbook.

## *Encourage Professional Development*

An increasing number of employees of various companies feel as if their contributions are not being noticed. They feel as if their efforts are being taken for granted. They want to be recognized, and they are in search of validation. All of this is not because they want attention, but because they want to be told whether their skill set is relevant and important. They wish to know whether or not their efforts are having a positive impact on the growth of the organization that they serve.

By definition, professional development is the
*"Process of improving and increasing the capabilities of staff through access to education and training opportunities in the workplace, through outside organization, or through watching others perform the job."*

It is vital that entrepreneurs and managers engage their loyal employees in order to ensure the success of their business. One of the most effective ways to retain employees is to continuously nurture their skills by providing employee development and training. This is not only beneficial for the company as it ensures a productive and skilled workforce, but also for the staff that is motivated and encouraged as a result of these development initiatives.

In order to be able to reduce the risk of losing top employees to the competition, leaders have to come up with plans of keeping their talented workforce on track. In today's cutting edge workplaces, businessmen need to understand that "one-size-fits-them-all" approach is no longer effective. The key to success lies in keeping the workforce on a constant-yet-steady road to development. Happy employees can do for a company what no one can.

A proper mindset is vital if employees are to benefit from any development programs in a company.

# THREE SECRETS TO PROMOTING SKILL DEVELOPMENT FOR BUSINESS RESULTS

Continuous participation is the key ingredient for the success of any employee development program. The challenges involved in keeping the employees engaged can be daunting to say the least. It is a fact that employees move, and their roles change. New employees have to be introduced to the company's skill measurement resources.

Without the participation of employees, the fate of any development strategy will be uncertain. That being said, it is absolutely vital that an initiative be taken to encourage employees to actively participate in their company's development programs.

The following should be considered whenever leaders attempt to encourage their employees and team members to develop and enhance their skill sets and abilities.

# Secret #1 – Establish and communicate skill goals

When the agenda for a professional development program is being established, it is absolutely vital to define clear goals for each of the participating employees. Depending on the extent of the training program, a business may opt to focus on a single skill at a given time, or they may even set benchmarks for a number of skills.

Regardless of whether the development programs are being launched for one skill, or a group of skills, it is of the utmost importance that clear goals be defined so that the staff has a clear picture of what they are expected to achieve. Setting a certain target also helps to bring all the participating members to the same skill level so that no one lags behind in their abilities. This goes a long way in developing a uniform, productive employee workforce that knows what the company expects from it.

Leaders may also assign certain "core" goals that all employees have to meet, then, once they have achieved those goals, they may be provided with customized training based on what their particular job role requires.

By assigning goals, a basic level of participation can be achieved. Yet, it is imperative that a clear message to all the participants be conveyed telling them that the defined goals are for the benefit of their skills development.

Periodic, personalized communication with each of the employees through whatever means preferred by a company can make a difference between a development program that lies dormant, and a program that yields ongoing results.

## Secret #2 – Define Milestones for Ongoing Development

After the employees have been assigned goals and have been engaged in a professional development initiative, it is essential that a direction for ongoing improvement is present, just like a ladder that can help employees rise with each step. This could take the form of assessment scores which the employees have to achieve in order to clear a particular milestone, or it could be the development of a new skill which would elevate their ranking in the development program. Such milestones can encourage participants to give their best and to participate with utmost determination.

A skills milestone, for instance, can be as straightforward as a specific deadline for finishing an assignment. A due date may not perhaps guarantee continuous development, but it can work effectively to promote engagement.

## Secret #3 – Know their achievements and boost morale

This is among one of the most useful factors that can greatly encourage professional development among a business's workforce. Recognizing achievements is the key to encouraging your employees, as it tells them that their efforts are being noted and appreciated. It also plays a critical role in engaging employees in a professional-development program, besides keeping them engaged to get maximum participation.

The question is: what is it that encompasses valid recognition?

An objective skills assessment score can provide compelling recognition. An employee may be appreciated and distinguished for achieving a certain percentile ranking by competing against a database of test-takers in a certain subject or skill. This can be a powerful motivator for self-development as well as professional development, particularly for the top-notch employees.

Other ways of recognition can be gained through methods such as certification of skills, high scores in projects, and by significantly improving weak skills.

## Assessing the need for training: Four simple steps

This process encompasses the assessment of the actual training needs of the organization. The training needs assessment is a process that aims to gather information regarding what kind of training needs exist in a company and what kind of training can assist the organization to accomplish its goals.

It is not uncommon to see many businesses implement training and development programs even before they conduct an employee skills assessment. There can be three outcomes as a result of this: the business may risk overdoing the training, it may provide too little training, or it may even miss the whole point of the training regime.

The following steps outline why it is essential to carry out an employee skill assessment, and the training needs assessment as a whole, before any development programs are initiated.

## Step 1 - Identification of problem areas

One of the major reasons why a training needs assessment must be carried out is because it helps to identify certain problem areas in a company. The Human Resources and the leadership team of a company must be aware of where the employees are lacking the required skills.

It is observed in many businesses that whenever an executive approaches the management team in order to request a training program, say on communication skills, the management simply gives a nod without even assessing whether this training is required or not. Too many times such cases lead to complete failure. The employees may consider the training program to be "good" and "informative," but as soon as they return to their usual work routines, no major change in productivity or increase in quality of work is observed. This is primarily because the training was not aimed at filling up the skill gaps; rather, it was more like shooting an arrow in the dark.

A more appropriate response by the management should have been to initiate an employee skill assessment in order to figure out whether a communication skills training program was needed or not.

## Step 2 - Get Management Support

It is surprising to see that even the management of many small businesses considers training to be a "nice thing to do," rather than considering it as an important step towards the development of their employees, and eventually the success of their business. In those organizational set-ups where managers are responsible for leading teams, the majority of times the best way to secure the management's support and confidence in launching training programs is by showing them how training can help the company reach its objectives more efficiently.

Whenever the management is shown solid proof that a certain employee-development program can enhance job performance, they will actively provide support and even encouragement. It will also prevent training programs from being eliminated as a result of budget cuts.

## Step 3 - Data Evaluation

Data concerning the needs for training and development of employees need to be collected before an actual training program is introduced. This data can then be compared with data collected after a training session to evaluate the engagement of employees and other participants.

## Step 4 - Determine Cost and Benefits of Training

Unfortunately, many organizations still consider training to be more of a nuisance rather than a contribution to the success of the business even though it is evident how employee training and development programs can contribute to the growth of the company.

The reason behind this belief can be attributed to the trainer's inability to present a cost-benefit analysis for the training program they carry out. It is obvious that hardly any employers would back away from a training program that costs the company $10,000, if that would correct a problem that is costing the company over $150,000 a year. That being said, the management may have to find the difference between the costs of no training against the cost of training in order to be able to take interest.

However, it is important that the management be aware of the fact that training is not the solution to each and every problem of the company, even though the later can drastically improve growth rates and morale of a company.

According to Huffington Post, over 77 percent of CEOs are worried about the lack of key skills, and over 60 percent say that skills gap makes it hard to fill the right positions in the company. This makes it clear that even though some employees may be occupying certain positions in a business, they may not have the sufficient skills and experience to fulfill the roles of their job wholly. In other cases, relocating employees from one position to another may also require brief training courses in order to make them suitable for the post.

Development and training for employees may be required in the following cases:

o Intern Training Plans
o New Employees
o New Managers
o Promotions

In many instances, such programs are often required to overcome certain organizational problems with the performance of employees, workplace safety, and production problems. In today's highly competitive industries, it is essential for a business to keep apprised of the changing needs of their clients and the industry as a whole. This requires that a company's workforce is trained on a regular basis in order to help them develop the ability to adjust to changing scenarios. Training may be essential as a result of the introduction of new technology, changes in the mission of the company, laws and regulations, etc.

As previously discussed, development is a major factor in boosting the morale and productivity of the employees. For the process to be successful, it needs to be carried out on three different levels: organizational, task, and individual.

## Organizational Analysis

An organizational analysis can be carried out to determine the areas that require training as well as to examine the conditions in which training will be conducted. It helps to identify the knowledge, skills, and the abilities which the employees will need in the coming future, particularly as their job or the company's objectives evolve. Analyzing this data can reveal the areas that require the maximum amount of improvement. For instance, the departments which have high turnover rates or particularly poor performance and productivity may be the first ones to be considered for skill development programs.

Whenever analyzing at this level, the leadership team needs to be able to answer questions such as how their business is changing, and how will this change affect their expectations of the workforce. Hence, future skill need of the company. Skill development becomes necessary whenever a company plans to install new technology and equipment for use by the employees. Without the appropriate training, inducting new equipment will result in no net gains in performance or productivity.

## Task Analysis

Task analysis requires that a comparison between the employees' current skills and their job descriptions be carried out in order for the training needs to be established. By reviewing the job descriptions, employers can directly establish individual goals for employees if they lack some of the skills needed to perform their job with maximum efficacy.

If any gaps are found between the performance of employees and their job descriptions, then this is indicative of the need for training.

## Individual Analysis

Individual analysis aims to target individual employees and analyzes their performance and productivity levels in whatever they do. This technique is probably the most important for small businesses as well as being the easiest because a small company may not have as many employees.

If this review brings to light any deficiencies, it will help the management figure out what kind of training and development courses are necessary to get rid of those deficiencies.

Surveys, interviews, and testing are among the most common and preferred ways of analyzing individual employees.

# Conducting a Successful Training Needs Assessment

In order to successfully conduct a training needs assessment on any of the three levels, it is vital to answer the following questions:

- What kind of problem needs to be addressed? Is it a lack of productivity, a lack of safety in the workplace, or any other problems affecting the performance of the employees?
- Have the training needs of the company been identified in the past? If so, how was the assessment carried out and what were the results?
- How much budget can be allocated for training and development of employees?

The duration and the depth of this assessment will depend on the individual needs of a business. Usually, all the data required can be collected by:

- o Posing surveys and questionnaires to the employees throughout the company hierarchy
- o Conducting interviews of the employees, either on an individual basis or as a group
- o Carrying out performance appraisals
- o Observing the performance and productivity of employees as and when they work on projects
- o Conducting tests to analyze the skills and knowledge of employees

Each of the methods will reveal a different kind of data with varying degrees of quality and quantity. I would suggest incorporating more than one method to collect data. For instance, a questionnaire may be followed up by an interview to see why individuals answered a question the way they did.

Moreover, before any particular training method is selected, it is important to answer the following questions:

## *What does the company hope to gain from this session?*

The training goals will vary from one scenario to another. However, in most cases, the training goals encompass the following:
- o  New Skills
- o  Improved Workplace Conduct
- o  Greater Safety at Work

## *Who is to be trained?*

It may be necessary to divide employees into groups depending on their current skill levels and the difficulty of the training. A business might have to conduct different sessions for:
- o  New Employees
- o  Experienced Employees
- o  Management

## *What is the training budget?*

The training budget will directly affect which training method a business chooses for their employees.

### *How much time has been allocated for training?*

The time that has been allocated for the training session will affect the selection of the training method. Some training methods and techniques will require more time than others.

Once these questions have been clearly answered, only then should the leadership team proceed and look into the choices that they have.

### *The Training Methods*

Even though technological improvements in the training industry have literally transformed the way training is done, I would strongly recommend the traditional training delivery options, as they still remain the most effective and viable methods.

# CHAPTER FOUR

# LINKING BUSINESS GOALS TO EMPLOYEE DELELOPMENT GOALS

In here you will find insight about how employee development and training can help businesses achieve strategic goals. It is not only about increasing employee productivity but also about improving the company's profitability scores. Moreover, you will find basic methods through which you can indulge your employees with business objectives, set specific training goals and make the most of this investment on your employees.

Employee development is synonymous with growth—an integral factor in job positions for most people. If development opportunities are not present in a given job position, the employees are likely to leave their organization after a short time period. It is a well-established fact which organizations all over the world have come to terms with since the previous decade. There are three ways to look at the concern at hand to further emphasize the importance of employee development. It is not just a personal incentive but equally important for business growth as well. This section covers all aspects of employee development in ample detail to justify its role in business enterprises.

## *The Relationship between Employee Development and Employee Retention*

As mentioned previously, about 18% of employee turnover is caused by lack of growth incentives. When employees see that their current job position does not hold any (further) opportunities for growth and development, they will look for opportunities to switch to other jobs with different organizations. This often leads your human resource into competitors' companies.

The relationship between employee development and employee retention is absolute. Most employees see employee training and development efforts as a symbol of care and concern. The organization is perceived as a caring organization where employees are valued and enriched. More often than not, employees will reciprocate these emotions and spend extended time periods in their employment status.

In fact, it is estimated that about 68% of employees that survive the first year of employment are likely to remain with the current employer if they feel connected with the organization. Training and development is the easiest means to achieve this end. Eventually, these percentages of employee retention can be converted into profitability scores for the company if the human resource is used wisely.

Development adds value to employee services. Not only this, it adds value to the employee as he/she becomes capable of handling complex tasks and projects. This is the kind of competency most companies seek. Regardless of this, people tend to respect their teachers and remain loyal to those who have played a part in career enrichment. This becomes the major driving force behind higher rates of employee retention.

If organizations are not playing their role in instigating emotions of concern and loyalty in their employees, they are eventually headed for extremely high turnover rates. Lack of development gives rise to dissatisfaction which is adequately reflected in their behaviors towards the organization.

The world today is changing at the speed of light. In a similar manner, the business dynamics keep evolving with each passing day. It is important to remain abreast with these changes in order to survive in the excessively competitive business environment. Any delays or irresponsiveness on behalf of a business can cost millions—an amount which is sufficient enough to threaten their survival. Well implemented Employee-development programs help in preparing employees for emerging challenges by improving their skills and knowledge. A needs assessment is conducted to identify the areas in which the employees need training and development.

Consequently, these weaknesses are overcome through targeted development efforts. This naturally helps in improving business competitiveness.

The key factor here is determining the problem areas and addressing them in a timely manner in order to achieve a competitive edge. If the businesses are quick in responding to arising needs inside the company as well as on the outside, they will prove to be a bigger challenge for competitors. Needless to say, business competitiveness is not only imperative for tackling competition but also for capitalizing on inherent opportunities and improving the company's profitability. It is turning into a survival instinct for most businesses.

Climbing the corporate ladder is a step by step process. At each stage of the ladder, the employee experiences a different set of ground realities and therefore needs a different skill set in order to perform the duties properly.

Employees gradually learn what their new job positions or job descriptions demand but the lag time is significant enough to cost the company dearly. Employee development is therefore a more viable option that prepares employees for their new roles. Consequently, the company's interests are preserved. As a result, employee development is associated with job enrichment as it allows employees to progress steadily through their careers. It opens opportunities for growth and advancement so the employees can assume bigger responsibilities within the organization. Such advancement is usually accompanied by a sense of accomplishment which keeps the employees motivated towards progress.

## How to Link Employee Development with Business Objectives

Contrary to popular belief, development efforts are not launched without a purpose. It is a carefully planned activity that aims to deliver a specific purpose. It is one of the rising trends in businesses these days.

About 90% of organizations believe development efforts are integral for important change initiatives within the company. A major portion of these are either already actively participating in development efforts for their employees or are likely to begin a similar initiative in the near future.

While some organizations try to perform these activities in house, most resort to outsourcing development initiatives for a wide array of reasons. Nevertheless, the basic framework that governs training and development programs in all organizations is centered on setting SMART objectives.

SMART is the acronym for "Specific, Measurable, Achievable, Real and Time-bound" goals. These five dimensions are essential to executing a successful learning campaign. It does not only keep the expectations of the management aligned with business objectives, but also makes them appreciate the improvements that emerge as a result of these efforts.

The aims for such programs are often based on improving employee productivity and hence the company's profitability. I have consulted with businesses inclined to follow popular trends as followed by competitors. I advise against such efforts as they are least likely to yield desirable results. The needs of all organizations are different. It is possible for a competitor to have a different set of training and development goals. Needs assessment highlights the problems faced by the organization in particular instead of the industry as a whole.

Now that we have established the importance of employee development, the next stage is to understand how to link it with business objectives in the most effective manner. Keep in mind that employee involvement in this regard is important. It does not only guarantee higher employee engagement but also greater job satisfaction and employee dedication.

## *Management by Objectives*

It is a comparably novel type of management style. It recognizes the labor force as humans instead of machines. Hence their participation is encouraged and appreciated. Moreover, this form of management believes in proactive decision making instead of reactive decision making. Employees work in collaboration with their employers to determine possible areas of improvement and work on it before the need arises. This means the organization as a whole is progressing ahead of its competition.

Admittedly, such initiatives are usually influenced by technological advancements or by competitor activities more than personal creativity. Nevertheless, this form of governance is known to yield better results than most other forms of management.

There are several benefits associated with management by objectives. The most important of these is the level of employee participation and the sincerity which the employers receive. When employees are entrusted with responsibilities, or when their opinions are heard and implemented, it gives them a certain sense of ownership. The employees feel valued, and heard, and thus become responsible to take their suggestions to the end. They feel accountable for the action, and will, therefore, put in maximum efforts to achieve said goals. It proves to be a bigger motivational factor to the employees than other intrinsic or extrinsic awards.

With this degree of involvement, loyalty towards the organization almost always follows. This means the employees are happier, and satisfied and, hence, less likely to look for other job opportunities. In effect, it reduces the turnover rate considerably.

Another important aspect of this form of management is the degree of autonomous decision making ability granted to employees. They have the right to use all resources available to them and pull in others that are needed in order to fulfill the business objective. They have the freedom to apportion and control business resources in a way that leads to desirable ends.

Although the employees will still be answerable to the senior management for their decisions, it nevertheless gives them a feeling of accomplishment. Instead of being overshadowed by the management, this gives an opportunity to average employees to shine and be noticed. The credit is rightfully delivered to the employees and not just to the management. Generally, supervising employees under management by objectives system is a little tricky. It is very different from traditional management and hence does not put the employees under direct supervision of managers. It needs a manager with leadership traits to make such an arrangement work productively. Otherwise, the plan can very well backfire with massive business and productivity losses.

At every stage of business operations, goals need to be set. This is how performance is measured, evaluated and planned.

Likewise, goals are set for all employees with respect to the work they are expected to deliver. The only difference between traditional management and management by objectives is the fact that it is not only the management who sets the targets. Instead, employees have an equal say while goals and targets are being set.

The goals are set in collaboration with employees during discussions or individual meetings. The employee has the full right to raise concerns and identify problems he may encounter while pursuing the course. The targets may be altered in view of these concerns. But once the goals are set, it becomes essential for the employee to meet these in order to keep up with the hierarchical progress.

During this, it is important for the management as well as the employee to be on the same page regarding the targets set. There should be no ambiguity or distrust during the exchange. Moreover, the goals need to be communicated well so that the employee is aware about what is expected from him/her over the next term. Setting goals or communicating them is not enough. The next step is to devise a strategy for implementation and to motivate the employees to achieve these goals.

## *Planning Implementation*

Work targets need to be set with forethought. They are not set for the short-term but rather for the long-term concerns of the organizations. Consequently, it may be possible for the employee to consider the said goals to be unachievable. It is up to the management to identify a possible course of action for each employee through which all targets will be met. This does not mean the management will be responsible for maintaining a strict supervision over the employees to make sure the plan is being followed. It simply intends to suggest the employees need to be told that the goals are achievable. They need to be shown a way to do so. If they perceive the targets to be too farfetched or unachievable, it will discourage them and they will end up not meeting their goals.

The planning needs to be factual. However, it should not be too elaborate or detailed. A certain level of autonomous decision-making opportunities needs to be maintained in the plan to let the employees feel in control. As a result, this will instill greater employee involvement.

Employees need not be told what they need to do and when. Instead, they should be given targets that they need to achieve. Whichever pathway they choose or however they get to their goals should be left upon their personal discretion.

## _Administering Accountability_

Naturally, if the employee is put in control of their work schedule and given certain tasks and targets that they need to meet, the upper management will need to keep a check and balance to make sure the independence is not being abused. This can be done by making the employees answerable for their progress. If yearly targets are set, a meeting should be conducted after a period of every three or four months. The objective of this meeting is to evaluate the progress till date and understand the future plan of action. Any rectifying measures can be taken to make sure the employees are headed in the right direction.

Even if desired results have not been achieved, it is important for the management to prompt the employee to share his/her ideas about future progress. They may have a better way to achieve results which the management fails to appreciate. Simply penalizing the employee for not meeting the said targets over the specified time period will only give rise to demotivation and non-creative thinking. It is important to keep the employee engaged for best results. After all, engaged employees can improve company productivity up to more than 200%.

While it is important for the employees to feel in control of their realm of expertise, this by no means should instill a sense of careless freedom. The employees need to be kept aligned with business objectives; their progress should be measured and they should be held accountable for their decisions. The management needs to stay passively in control to keep the organizational structure intact.

## *Orchestrating the Process*

Management by objectives revolves around employee participation and a dormant management. The employees manage themselves for greater goals without the direct influence of management. The manager needs to play the role of a mentor and a leader instead of a supervisor. The idea is to make the unit self-sufficient but within the prescribed limits. While the process is being carried out, the management should be available to assist the employees in their tasks. However, they need not be actively involved in it. Employees need to be supervised without being made to feel the same. Excessive control over employee actions can be seen as an intrusion on their private space which will eventually lead to dissatisfaction.

The idea behind this strategy is to help employees learn managerial skills. It aims to instill leadership qualities in the employees so they can exhibit their true potential for the organization's benefit. At a later date, it will be possible for organizations to recruit managers internally for best results.

In other words, the management needs to be orchestrating the whole progress without becoming evident. Their involvement should not be too obvious yet their absence should not be felt. Employees need to be given freedom yet within a specified limit. It is all about managing two extremes for results that reciprocate business objectives.

## *Measuring Progress*

Setting SMART goals makes measuring progress easier. SMART goals are accompanied by key performance indicators (KPIs) which help you quantify progress in an unbiased manner. The management and the employees both need to be fully knowledgeable about these evaluation factors to ensure fair appraisals.

In terms of sales, the most obvious key performance indicator is the number of sales made. It can also be quantified by the number of customer grievances that were handled professionally or the number of repeat customers. Moreover, the same can also be measured by customer feedback collected through surveys, focus groups, or otherwise. More than one key performance indicator can also be used to evaluate employee performance. However, the employee needs to be aware of all dimensions on which his/her performance is being judged.

Each dimension should be given a particular weightage which will be used to compute the final score. Based on this, the future plan of action will be devised and implemented.

Management by objectives is an effective mode of management from several perspectives. It does not only ensure employee engagement but also does so with respect to business objectives. Over time as the company progresses, this technique helps in keeping employees actively involved with the organizational decision making process so they are less inclined to feeling worthless or dissatisfied. This impacts employee retention as well as employee development positively. It keeps the focus of employee development and training efforts aligned with business goals so that greater ends can be achieved.

Management by objectives is known to yield higher job satisfaction scores. Generally, people don't like to be bossed around. Management by objectives ensures they feel the same without actually being their own bosses! It is a perception which works well for organizations as well as for employees.

# Integrity of Performance Reviews – What it means to your business

While everyone might all agree that performance reviews are vital to enforcing accountability, I have come across many organizations which either don't have them, only do them at the managerial level and ignore the rest of the staff, do not know how to do them, and therefore use them only to point out faults in employee performance.

This also is a process that should be supported by senior management. At the same time, I urge every manager, supervisor, and business leader and HR professional to refrain from utilizing a performance appraisal as a tool for punishment. When used incorrectly, not only does it not help improve performance, it also contributes to low morale and attrition in the work place. Your HR department may not see anything wrong with that practice (which they often favor) and advocate it as a way of getting rid of poor performers. In a well planned development program, poor performers will be identified early and know where they stand before the time for review.

Employees like to feel appreciated and valued. Performance review is a way to acknowledge the workforce for their time, dedication and quality of work. As long as they are aware that they are headed in the right direction, they will be more inclined to progress steadily. It is one of the essentials pertaining to employee retention. Employer's feedback keeps employees involved with their work so they are less likely to think about leaving their jobs. About 94% of organizations across the world indulge in performance appraisals and feedback. However, almost half of the workforce (48%) believes the performance appraisal programs are not working well and hence need to be improved.

It is important for performance appraisals to be extremely fair, unbiased and constructive. Employees have certain expectations with their performance appraisals and their managers. 70% of the employees hope to see a performance review that will guide them towards growth and development. 22% of the employees see it as recognition to stay put. 8% of the employees hope the review will include a discussion that will help address his/her problems effectively.

Contrary to this, most employees fail to see what they expect and will eventually feel discouraged to work in the same place. Sadly, 51% of the employees see performance reviews as inaccurate. Consequently, 53% of employees feel less motivated to work harder or progress. Eventually, these employees become twice as likely to seek employment elsewhere as soon as they receive results from their appraisers.

While a performance review is an integral portion of employee involvement, if employers fail to do so appropriately, it will eventually lead to bigger problems including job dissatisfaction and high employee turnover.

58% of the managers feel they are offering ample amounts of feedback and reviews for their employees. In contrast to this, 65% of employees feel they need more feedback to truly assess their potential and performance.

Feedback and appraisals are directly linked with employee engagement. If provided the right feedback and at the right time, employees can be engaged in their tasks in a much better manner. 90% of the employees believe reviews and feedback based on positivity and achievements are seen as greater motivators than negative feedback. On the other hand, positive feedback has the capacity to increase employee engagement up to 50 times as compared with an employee who receives no or negligible feedback.

On the same note, it is important to realize that employees are looking for a personalized approach to performance reviews. They need adequate recognition for all their works and achievements instead of a software generated piece of paper that delivers the same set of advice and scores to all employees. Performance appraisals that lack a human touch will be seen as an indicator of the fact that the company has no time to value its employees.

If appraisals are delivered by someone other than the immediate manager, it raises concern in employees about the validity of the reviews. Since the new appraiser has never witnessed the work ethics of employees firsthand, s/he is likely to be relying on second hand information which may lack certain important aspects. Due to this, such appraisals can greatly discourage employees to work diligently towards their goals.

Inability to acknowledge past achievements is also seen as a discouraging factor. About 22% of the employees feel upset with their performance appraisals because they fail to recognize past achievements. Resultantly, the center of focus for such appraisals is usually incompetence and missed targets. Negative feedback rarely ever helps employees in any way. In fact, 21% of employees consider their performance appraisals outright demeaning.

Another important concept to keep in mind is the fact the employees detest singular points of view when it comes to performance appraisals. 40% of employees are dissatisfied with their appraisals because they come from a single source—the manager—who might not even be actively involved with the employees. For the most part, these employers will be unaware of employee challenges and hence unable to provide an unbiased view for appraisals. 73% of the employees see peer to peer performance reviews as preferable. This is because this method incorporates feedbacks from other employees going through the same set of challenges. This takes into account the environmental factors influencing performance and sets realistic expectations.

Crowd sourced feedback is another recent development in appraisals. Instead of relying on a single source of information, it collects information from multiple resources and then combines them to get an aggregate score. 80% of the employees feel more satisfied with this form of review. It makes about 88% of the employees feel satisfied with their jobs as compared with 67% of employees undergoing traditional appraisals.

The frequency of appraisals and reviews also matters for the employees. They need timely recognition and feedback to keep their pace aligned with business objectives. 71% of the employees claim they would like to receive feedback for their projects immediately or as soon as possible. 23% of employees feel that weekly appraisals are as likeable as immediate feedbacks. Only 17% of the employees feel satisfied at quarterly or annual appraisals. Time is therefore a crucial factor in determining employee satisfaction.

The crux of the story is that performance appraisals and reviews help employees stay motivated towards their goals. At the same time, reviews coming from a single, uninvolved source are not received well by the employees.

As mentioned at the beginning of this book, I am a firm advocate of ongoing coaching and development practices in the workplace. Simply because they alleviate, if not eliminate, this notion of noninvolvement from supervisors and managers. It allows them to collaborate and agree on common goals, which the employee is empowered to help create and be held accountable for. (I will cover this concept of workplace coaching in more details in my next book).

The 360 degree performance or peer review technique often offers some sense of false hope to the employee being evaluated. I refer to it as such simply because if the organizations don't take the time to educate peers on the value of feedback, as far as why it's done and how to receive it, it will do more harm than good. I have worked with organizations where 360 degree peer reviews are very painful to assimilate, with HR and leadership having no involvement nor offering any guidance in the process. Or simply initiated if and when the employee asks to be evaluated, at times in an attempt to justify getting a raise or promotion. If your organization seeks to use this process, I urge you to differ.

## *360 Degree Performance Review and Appraisals*

A 360 degree performance review and appraisals scheme should aim to overcome the weaknesses of most traditional evaluation platforms. Instead of a single source of review, this strategy makes use of all possible ways to receive feedback. Each medium is assigned a certain weightage which is then used to evaluate the final scores. This reduces the chance for biased reviews or unfair appraisals. About 90% of Fortune 500 companies are known to employ the 360 degree performance appraisal technique. It does not only take into account the feedback from immediate managers and supervisors but also includes peer reviews. 43% of employees value peer review more as compared with manager's reviews.

Peer reviews can work wonders when it comes to job satisfaction, employee retention and employee engagement. About 88% of the employees feel more satisfied with their jobs when they are peer reviewed as compared with 67% of employees feeling satisfied with manager-reviewed appraisals. Moreover, 76% of employees feel this form of evaluation should be formally added to performance reviews.

These days, about 89% of organizations link pay decisions with performance reviews to keep employees motivated. Despite this, only 42% of the organizations are actually known to track this relationship and keep it adequately aligned with company benchmarks. This has also become a leading factor for employee turnover and disengagement.

On the whole, 360 degree performance appraisals bridge the gap in the traditional model of evaluation and are therefore well received by most employees. It gives a chance to eliminate errors and biases. Moreover, it keeps the employees motivated towards subsequent goals. If done properly, it can be used as a tool to improve employee retention and engagement.

## _Individual Performance Improvement Strategies_

Teamwork rules the current decade; it is common for employers to review teams collaboratively as compared with individuals. However, the need to fix the missing link becomes even more pronounced when it comes to improving team performance.

Employees feel more valued when they are evaluated individually and on a personal level. Sadly, about

90% of the employers and managers fail to establish a personal connection with their employees. Most employers face minimal or no employee participation when it comes to appraisals, goal setting, development planning, and so on and so forth. Consequently, employees lack the motivation they need to excel at their targets and outperform benchmarks. Only 14% of employers actively indulge in discussions with employees to evaluate performance. On the other hand, only 8% of employers welcome employee concerns overall goals setting. Such practices lead to employee demotivation as 70% of the employees hope to see positive feedback and improvement opportunities during reviews.

The use of software to develop performance reviews was another major disaster that occurred previously. Most employees would be rated as an average and would therefore receive more or less the same reviews. Consequently, employees began to see it as a symbol of carelessness on behalf of the employers. Direct personal feedback is therefore essential for employee development.

## *Management Feedback*

The management needs to be evaluated just as much as the managed ones. It is important for managers to take time out of their busy schedules to interview the employees and find out about their problems and challenges. These factors need to be taken into consideration while evaluating their performance to make the employees feel they have been justified.

In general, 58% of managers believe they offer sufficient feedback to their employees. 34% believe they could offer more valuable feedback if they were given the time. In contrast with this, only 35% of employees feel they receive ample feedback. 65% of employees feel they need more feedback in order to ensure their progress is aligned with business objectives. This gap in manager services and employee expectations has the potential to transform into a major drawback for the company. Management feedback implies employees' views about their immediate supervisors are heard. This, in turn, makes it possible to achieve greater strategic collaboration between employees and management.

## *Face-to-Face Performance Appraisal*

The importance of face-to-face appraisal cannot be stressed enough. It is infinitely better than a piece of paper forwarded to let employees know how they are performing. About 78% executives reported they exhibit higher dedication to performance management when they indulge in one-on-one performance discussions. About 70% employees are likely to feel more satisfied with their appraisals if they are conducted in person and they are based on quantitative goals and improvements. 65% of employees claimed they seek ways to improve their performance as the primary part of their appraisals, though

80% of the appraisals are considered inadequate at providing this basic need.

Face-to-face appraisals open windows for dual communication. The employee has as much right to contribute towards the discussion as the employer. Hence the result is a better, well-rounded collaborative effort that not only addresses weaknesses but also devises strategies to overcome these.

In another research it was concluded that appreciation by an immediate supervisor is considered a bigger motivator as compared with cash bonuses. Recognition programs can help improve business outcomes by 12 times.

About 31% of employees feel their bosses do not appreciate them or value them adequately. Hence they feel less motivated towards work. This discrepancy can easily be resolved through face-to-face interactions between the management and the employees. If the employees feel heard, valued and involved, they are likely to exhibit positive characteristics. This eventually translates into greater engagement and hence better progress towards business objectives.

These are just three straightforward, result-driven appraisal techniques I often recommend. There are practically a million things employers can do to make their employees feel valued, motivated and engaged with business goals. In the long run, the businesses have a lot to benefit from productive employees.

# Evaluating Productivity through Performance Appraisals

Performance appraisals of employees are a vital tool in the development and career progression of all the employees. If a company is establishing training and development programs for its employees, then it is imperative that a performance management system be put in place to assist in the employees' career development. One of the best ways of developing and enhancing the skills and abilities of an employee is when managers regularly coach and mentor them. The conventional view of employee development based on what goes on in a classroom is constricted.

In order to be able to effectively broaden the horizon of the workforce and to keep the employees motivated to ensure maximum productivity and benefits for the company, it is essential that a business fully understands the actual meaning of performance management.

## Defining Performance Management

Great effort has been taken by HR professionals and specialists to define performance management. Without going into too much detail, performance management refers to the *continuing* communication between a supervisor and an employee. To get the most effectual results, the process should involve establishing clearly-defined goals and targets for the employee under consideration. The job responsibilities of both the employee and the manager should be discussed so that the employee is fully aware of how he or she is expected to work as a team.

Note the emphasis on the word "continuing" in the previous paragraph. It is not sufficient to review the performance of an employee only on an annual basis. To ensure optimal performance management, I often recommend quarterly or semi-annual reviews.

If the performance management system is to be used as an effective tool for the development of employees, the feedback provided to the staff must be immediate. It is not wise to save all the feedback and dump it on the employee during an annual performance review. The best results are achieved when a supervisor points out the shortcomings of an employee and helps him or her to overcome them; particularly when the employee is stuck with a problem. Feedback provided on a timely basis has long-lasting effects due to the fact that the learning is usually applied immediately.

The management of a company can assess the ability and performance of the supervisors themselves to see how well they are managing the employees. An easy way is to gather a group of small employees and ask them how they know when they are doing the job well. In the majority of the cases, the answer that comes is "when we don't hear anything." This is unfortunate, but true; after all, we must not forget that praise goes a long way in motivating employees and encouraging them to work harder, thus increasing the productivity in both the short and long term.

## *The Performance Review*

A performance review is a vital component of a performance management system. For quite some time, there has been a difference of opinion regarding the effectiveness of formal performance reviews among business executives. According to W. Edward Deming, performance reviews can bring little good to an organization, and the potential for de-motivating employees through a performance review is far greater than the benefits.

However, it is becoming clear that constructive feedback in a performance review can work wonders in encouraging employees to perform at their best by continuously improving. This makes performance reviews an important part of the performance management system.

## *The Criteria for Appraising Performance*

The criteria for reviewing performance must always be based on the job responsibilities and duties of each position in the company. If the supervisor does not have a detailed outline of the job descriptions, a person from the human resources department must provide them with the list of people and the responsibilities of their positions.

Once this information has been gathered, a performance review form can be designed that suits the structure and the working of the organization. While it may seem the easiest thing to do, downloading a pre-designed review form from the Internet is generally not recommended because it may not be based on the criteria applicable to the business's job descriptions. Generic forms will not be as effective as custom-designed ones. When assessing the performance of the individual employees, the criteria that are used must be depicted in measurable and behavioral terms.

*Measurable:* Measurable performance criteria refer to quality, speed of delivery, quantity, and the profitability of a project or projects. Some managers argue that their work is not measurable; however, how is it then that they measure the success of their work?

*Behavioral:* These are the actions that have been observed or corrected through coaching or any other means.

## Designing a Performance Appraisal Process

This section contains a brief outline of how the leadership team can go about designing and implementing the process of performance appraisals in their organization.

1. *Designing the Process:* The Human Resources personnel are responsible for designing the appraisal process with inputs and help from the management. If the leadership team does not provide sufficient support, or if it feels that a performance review system is of a little or no value, it is most likely that the system will fail in its early stages.

2. *Training of Employees:* It is often observed that both the supervisors and employees view performance appraisals as a painful process. The supervisors, in their "judgmental seat," are usually uncomfortable; while the employees under scrutiny may become defensive. This is why it's important for both the supervisors and the employees to receive training if this mindset is to be changed to good.

The performance appraisal has to be transformed into an effective and smooth process. The supervisors must be provided training so that they know how to communicate the appraisal to the employees and so that they can observe the behavior. Furthermore, it is also important that employees be told the importance of performance appraisals and how they should receive the feedback constructively.

3. *Distribution of Forms:* Once the supervisors have been trained on how to carry out performance appraisals, the performance review forms are distributed among the managers and supervisors so

that they can report the performance of each of the employees.

4. *Talking about Performance:* This is the next step involved a meeting between the supervisor and the employee in order to discuss their performance over certain duration. The results of the appraisal should be handed to the employee, with one copy going to the HR department. The supervisor also assigns targets which the company expects the employee to achieve until the next performance review.

A performance appraisal, if designed correctly, can be a powerful motivational tool that can help enhance the productivity of the workforce, which, in essence is vital for the growth of a business.

# CHAPTER FIVE

# THE VALUE OF REWARDS AND RECOGNITION AND ITS IMPACT ON BUSINESS RESULTS

Employee recognition is not simply a nice thing that should be done to praise employees. It is actually a very important communication tool that helps to reinforce and reward people for what they do for a company. Whenever a company recognizes its employees, it reinforces their actions and encourages them to continue contributing for the success of the company.

An effective recognition and reward system within a business equips the workforce with three key elements:

1. It offers them a fair return for their hard work and efforts
2. It motivates them to maintain and enhance their performances
3. It reinforces their actions and sets an example for other employees

To effectively capitalize on the benefits of such programs, companies should:

## _Involve Employees_

One of the best ways to encourage people to perform better is by involving them in designing the recognition and reward program. This way, they will know what they have to do to earn rewards and recognition.

## _Determine Reward Criteria_

Awards can be given out on numerous instances; for innovation, showing initiative, and for improvement in quality are common instances in this regard. However, quite often it is observed that the staff does not know what needs to be done in order to gain that reward. Without such information, employees will not have a clear picture of what is being encouraged. Thus, it is necessary that a business clearly sets the criteria for each of the rewards.

## _Reward Everyone_

Everyone who meets the reward criteria should be awarded. A fair recognition and reward system will ensure that the performance of all people is noted without any favoritism or luck. It is best to offer several types of awards, with each of them having their own set of criteria.

What would be the point of having a single winner at the end of each month, with others feeling that their hard work for the whole month was simply wasted?

## *Acknowledge Behavior Along With Outcomes*

In the majority of businesses, results lead to rewards. Not that there is something wrong with this method, but it doesn't reduce the opportunity to utilize recognition as a way to persuade low performers to improve.

If the management pays attention to even the slightest behavioral improvements, such as arriving on time to work, correcting mistakes as well as helping other employees— then the person should be recognized for this. Even a simple "Thank You" can go a long way in acknowledging someone.

## *Nurture Self-Esteem*

Whenever employees are given positive and realistic feedback on their efforts, accomplishments, the potential which they have, as well as their self-esteem improves. They gain confidence and become motivated enough to work harder for the company. Praise is a vital factor that is necessary for the development of confident, productive employees.

## *How the Job Market Sees It*

Most graduates entering the job market and searching for employment opportunities come in with a mindset. They intend to grow with time and experience. So even if they accept corporate exposure at entry-level, they intend to develop core competencies and prerequisite skill sets over time through this association to progress upwards on the corporate ladder.

Employee development and growth is defined as the transition from entry-level job positions to senior ranks over time and with adequate training to ensure the responsibilities of senior managerial levels are delivered properly. It is the key contributing factor towards job satisfaction.

It is estimated that about 18% of employee turnover is attributed to lack of career advancement and employee development. This turnover rate is, by and large, preventable if adequate opportunities are provided. Since voluntary terminations of employees depict a consistently increasing trend, it has raised concerns for organizations all over the world.

Companies that lack a proper framework to determine career progress experience highest turnover rates. Employees like to evolve and assume newer responsibilities over time that can contribute to their growth.

Employees see training and development efforts on behalf of the company as an attempt to retain employees. It is a major investment on the human resources of a company to nourish and polish their skills according to the needs of their jobs. Progress is accompanied with newer challenges and hence needs an advanced set of skills to be tackled the right way.

Employee development and growth is the first step towards in-house recruitment for superior job positions. This reduces the time needed by a new employee to acclimatize with "new" company standards. This ensures the vacancy can be filled in a timely manner and also that the losses incurred during the transitory phase can be kept to a minimum.

The job market comprises of several thousands of fresh graduates each year who see this as a major attraction in any job position with any organization. In fact, it is rated as the number one concern by most graduating students.

About 54% of students entering the job market have employee development and career progress in mind. They are more likely to settle for low-paying jobs if they can perceive adequate career progress over the years. On the other hand, most high-paying job positions are likely to experience a similarly high turnover rate due to lack of accomplishment and progress.

The need for progress surpasses the importance of remuneration and leadership. According to a survey, employees who believed they would switch their jobs if they were offered better compensation plans by a competitor, were given a better work-life balance, or were able to see better opportunities for progress. However, those who did switch their jobs admitted their first and foremost concern included better opportunities for progress. Compensation took the last place in this regard. This adequately summarizes the ongoing trends in the job market and the importance of progress in the eyes of employees.

On the other hand, it has been noted that the human resource departments in several companies are facing difficulty finding the right candidates for intricate jobs. At times, the companies will have to suffer losses for up to three months at a stretch due to the inadequacy of applicants. Training and employee development is the only way to convert this segment into productive employees.

On a similar note, it is worthy of mention that today's education system is not capable of transferring basic skills and expertise to students. Although such institutions unarguably work well while providing theoretical knowledge and framework, they are deficient in tutoring people about the practical implications of such theories. So, while most graduates will have a good idea about management, they seldom know how or what needs to be done.

# The Pay Factor – How does it affect Development and Business Objectives?

The business environment these days is extremely competitive. While there are few disparities in terms of products and services offerings from different companies, the focus of differentiation has shifted to employee retention instead.

Human resource has emerged as an unparalleled strength for all organizations irrespective of their industry or size. Thus employee retention and employee growth has received noteworthy emphasis in recent years. Business results cannot be achieved without the support and collaboration of a united workforce that aims to deliver the same. Gone are the days when administering employee discipline used to be linked with remuneration. These days "job satisfaction" has found an integrated meaning pertaining to several aspects of work life—salaries are a small part of it.

*One of the HR Managers in my advisory program, who works in the retail industry mentioned to me that she had to constantly meet with her outsourced recruiting agency and is currently on the verge of firing them because her turnover rates are sky high. The candidates that are sent to them are very lazy, always late to work and eventually stop showing up within a week of being hired. No data have been collected on why the employees are always late, nor the real reason why they stop coming altogether. The department managers have concluded that a perfect solution would be to use a different agency for better results, offer more money in order to bring in better candidates, and encourage referrals from current employees. All of which have been implemented, except changing the agency, and, of course, the retention issue still persists.*

*My answer —It pays to know what the real cause of a problem is before taking action. My recommendation was to complete a climate survey focusing on the specific issues that seem to be the problem, in order to identify the next course of action. If management was to be the problem, they would never point the finger at themselves and say we need to do a better job at ensuring retention, not to mention, in that particular organization meeting retention goals is the sole responsibility of the HR department. Sure enough, in the results 80% of the employees admitted that communication around work hours and expectations are poor or nonexistent, 72% rated the leadership skills of their immediate supervisors as poor, only 60% say they would recommend that employer to a family member, out of which only 25% would recommend it as long-term employment. Only 23% of those surveyed indicated that they were not satisfied with their current pay rate.*

*My recommendation was for her to share the results with the senior leadership team, and work on a long-term plan for intervention. Ideally, this is a process that would need to be spearheaded and supported by senior leaders in demanding full accountability from lower level managers and supervisors in order to be successful.*

I reference this case to say the following,

An unsatisfied employee is least likely to maintain his/her position with the current company irrespective of the salary structure. It is estimated that 1 in every 2 employees is dissatisfied with his/her job and is therefore likely to become a part of the job searching segment within a year. According to a recent research conducted with over 7944 respondents from different universities, about 54% expressed that career development and growth is their number one concern while searching for jobs. As they graduate to enter the job market, organizations should anticipate a growth-oriented mindset of their workforce in the near future.

This aims to emphasize the importance of career growth and advancement in the eyes of the employees. This, by no means, aims to undermine the importance and influence of salaries on employee decisions. Admittedly, about 47% of employees are known to be dissatisfied with their jobs owing to their salary structures. Inadequate compensation can lead to higher turnover rates. It is important to strike a balance between these two aspects in particular and all aspects of job satisfaction in general to promote healthy employment practices.

Recognizing these changing trends is vital to business growth and we have therefore come up with the concept of talent management. It aims at not only recognizing talent in employees but also at nourishing and promoting them for greater business gains.

## *The Concept of Talent Management*

Talent management is a relatively novel concept that revolves around the recruitment, retention, development and compensation of employees aligned with strategic workforce planning. The underlying principle helps human resource managers plan their hiring routines in accordance with the changing business needs. Moreover, it also aims to reduce the time lag to a minimum—any vacancy created should be filled immediately so that business processes are not hampered.

The process of hiring new employees is a lengthy and expensive feat. It is even trickier to gain access to experienced employees that can join the work force immediately. Especially at managerial level, the importance of employee retention cannot be stressed enough. Such positions are extremely sensitive for business profitability. The vacancy can cost the business dearly in terms of revenues and productivity losses and also in terms of hiring and recruitment efforts needed to access a specialized work force segment.

Alternatively, helping employees realize opportunities for career advancement and growth can play a pivotal role in employee retention. An employee who can see consistent career progress is more likely to stay with an organization (even with a small salary package).

High salary packages can unarguably attract a hefty bulk of CVs but the employee retention tends to decline. Once the imminent needs are fulfilled, employees need intrinsic sources of satisfaction to continue with their progress. This is the biggest missing part of the puzzle that most organizations fall prey to. An average graduate these days is likely to pursue 7 career paths during his/her course of life. This further highlights the importance of job satisfaction to inculcate loyalty towards an organization. More so, this highlights the importance of hiring the right people for the right job—an integral portion of talent management.

Talent management revolves around the concept of retaining employees that fulfill integral key roles in a business concern or are likely to do the same in near future. Today's executives have to be able to use these resources to predict current and future human resource needs and the development of strategies to meet these needs. Talent management is integral to business success as it focuses on one of the most important aspects of organizational operations—labor.

The relationship between employee development and employee retention is absolute. If employees do not feel they are constantly moving towards progress, their morale declines and so does their willingness to stay with their current employer. On the other hand, employee development is surely linked with higher employee retention and job satisfaction.

About 39% of employees are motivated to stay in their current employment if they can adequately comprehend opportunities for career growth. Similarly, 32% employees feel happy with their job position and organization if they are constantly faced with opportunities to develop their skills and expertise in their area of interest. This clearly points towards employees needs for constant progress and development.

## *Are they in for Learning or Money (Or Both)?*

Most employees acquire jobs for learning as well as to gain financial independence. It is difficult to pinpoint a singularly most important factor because most people have mixed opinions. Different people are motivated by different aspects. So it is safe to assume both are equally important when it comes to employee motives. However, extensive research has been done to identify how people perceive their association with companies, especially those who have graduated recently and are preparing to join the job market. It was observed that about 54% of the respondents considered career advancement opportunities as the foremost concern in maintaining employment with their organization. In contrast with this, only 51% respondents believed their salaries were integral to their association. 51% believed they would stay with their employers if their work was challenging and interesting. People these days focus more on career progress than monetary benefits. Admittedly the latter is equally important when it comes to compensating high performers. Nevertheless, most people actually switching over to other jobs or other companies are really doing so for progress rather than compensation.

## *Evaluating Development Focus against Salary Orientation*

Employees all over the world have a distinctive growth and development focus instead of salary-orientation in making employment decisions. Most of the new entrants in the job market do so with a predefined mindset which puts growth ahead of remuneration. Also, most people who have enjoyed impressive pay structures have also come to terms with the importance of growth and development. For most people, the possibility of growth is what determines their length of employment at a specific organization.

When and if employees are forced to perform the same activities and functions day after day, it causes mental burn out and redundancy. People lose interest in their tasks and look elsewhere to challenge their creative spark. This is the first step towards employee disengagement and loss of productivity. In this case, no amount of benefits or compensation leverages can help the company retain a progressively disengaged employee.

## What Can Businesses Do?

I have witnessed this way too often when companies throw a raise at a dissatisfied worker who's threatening to leave. Or feel compelled to throw more money at someone whose skill sets are not bringing much value to the organization. In either case, these actions serve as a temporary fix. The simplest thing to realize and appreciate is that compensation is a small part of job satisfaction; there are several other factors that contribute towards employee happiness other than salary. Businesses need to understand how human resource psyche workers to improve their work environment, promote employee engagement and reduce employee turnover.

There are a few things that employees can forego (remuneration for instance) and a few that they absolutely need (sense of accomplishment). Organizations need to understand what their workforce values and what they can overlook. It is important for a manager to take time out of business concerns to find out and understand what their employees are thinking and doing. Organizations can make major improvements to their work environment as well as to their governance policies if they know what employees need. If the employees feel heard, valued, and honored, they are less likely to switch elsewhere. Failure to do so, however, cannot bring about any positive change in the organization. Feedback exchange has to happen both ways so that the management as well as the workforce is aware of what is expected of them and what they need to do. Businesses should begin by being all ears to hear employee concerns. The rest will automatically fall into place.

## Benefits of a Development Focus – 7 Reasons why it yields better business results

Development focus is not just important from the employee's perspective. In fact, organizations can also benefit greatly from this mindset.

Here are seven reasons to help organizations see why employee development is imperative for business success. Employee Development through learning and through career progress plays a pivotal role in employee enrichment. It is synonymous to progress—which is singularly the most important factor for job satisfaction. Employee enrichment helps organizations greatly. Not only does this mean employees are learning about newer technologies and market trends, it also means the company is gaining a competitive advantage over contending firms. The company can make use of this skilled asset and turn their contributions into profits.

Development efforts aim to equip employees with the latest from their respective fields. It upgrades their skill sets, knowledge and expertise and aligns it with current industry practices. Consequently, employees are able to improve their performance. Employee development is a way to promote a culture of learning within the organization. Acquiring more skills and knowledge is also a symbol of progress. As people find out newer and better ways to conduct business, they are able to take organizational objectives to a wholly different level. It prevents employees from becoming obsolete, unproductive, or stagnant. If anything, the workforce as well as the business keeps moving forward.

## The 7 Reasons

### *Reason #1 - Consistent Improvement*

If organizations indulge in development efforts frequently, it plays an important part in improving business operations at a consistent pace.

As employees readily familiarize themselves with new and improved methods of conducting business and performing their duties, the product of their efforts gets improved. Consequently, it does not only play a pivotal role in business competitiveness but also in organizational progress.

Businesses that fail to invest in development efforts put their employees in a delusional comfort zone. Employees are misled into believing they are performing their duties well when in fact they fail to meet the desired level of productivity.

As more processes become automated and mechanized, it is possible to improve business productivity multifold. Those organizations not making adequate use of technology or not being able to remain up-to-date with the recent advancements are not capitalizing on this opportunity. They lag behind and eventually end up being engulfed by the competition. The business environment of the modern era is more dynamic than ever before. Failure to stay abreast with the latest occurrences can put companies at an extreme disadvantage. Hence the importance of employee development from the organizational point of view cannot be adequately stressed when it comes to employee enrichment.

## *Reason #2 - Employees Feel Cared For*

Progress and development is an intrinsic need for most people. They do not like serving in the same role and performing the same duties for years at stretch. Change keeps the creative spark intact while also ensuring the employee potential is put to full use. For this reason, most people perceive employee development and training efforts on behalf of organizations as a means to show they care for their workforce. They value those who work for them and hence try to enhance this value by consistent training efforts. It is an investment that companies make on their employees to help them outperform their goals and hence cherish a sense of achievement.

If employees feel valued, they will automatically reciprocate these emotions positively. This becomes evident in their performance scores.

## *Reason #3 - High Loyalty and Dedication*

Employees who feel cared for are likely to spend longer time periods with their employers. It is a natural response exhibited by most people. They tend to be more loyal towards the organization, more dedicated towards their goals and more willing to become top performers. Needless to say they have the potential to become unparalleled assets for the company. About 41% of employees in companies which do not possess adequate training and development programs are likely to leave the organization within one year. This is because such an institution lacks the fundamental aspect of job satisfaction—progress.

On the other hand, in case where adequate training and development opportunities are present, the employee retention score can be improved substantially. Only 12% of employees are likely to part ways with their employers despite growth opportunities. This clearly summarizes the role of development and progress in inculcating loyalty and commitment in employees.

## *Reason #4 - Elevated Productivity*

Training and development equips employees with the latest technologies and skills which can be put to use to instill competitiveness. Consequently, with the latest industry operations, employees can increase their individual productivity as well as that of their company's. Elevated productivity is considered synonymous to increased profitability for the company.

Research has shown that employees feel they are being unproductive for about 38% of their time spent at their workplace—about 17 hours in a typical 45 hours-per-week schedule. This feeling may stem from a number of reasons including infrastructural problems, lack of guidance, lack of definitive goals, and others. However, 60% of the employees take the feeling of being unproductive back home which contributes towards the work-life imbalance and further worsens the case.

When employees feel unproductive, it leads to other problems for the organization. For instance, it reduces their morale so they feel less inclined to invest in improving their processes. They feel disengaged and aloof from organizational decisions, which contributes towards job dissatisfaction. Eventually, such employees become twice as likely to switch their jobs when contrasted against other reasonably engaged employees. Not only this, low morale and employee disengagement costs organizations their profitable and competitive status as well. About 22 million employees experience low morale. This in turn incurs productivity losses up to $350 billion per year across different businesses. This figure can easily be improved if companies become apt at investing in adequate training and development efforts in a timely manner.

When employees become aware of better ways to conduct business, they will automatically reduce their unproductive hours to a minimum. They will feel more motivated to work harder as they see their performance indicators soar visibly higher. Not only this, but they will also feel personally involved in the business which will affect their confidence levels outside the workplace positively. The scheme works both ways—if employees feel happy and satisfied with their jobs, they are likely to work hard and hence make more profits for the company. At the same time, if the employees feel frustrated, anxious, or unproductive, it will automatically begin to reflect in their performance.

## Reason #6 - Employees Feel Valued and Involved

If training and development efforts are well coordinated within the employee base, the results can be greatly improved. This means the training needs assessment should be carried out while keeping the employee concerns in mind. Also, repeating the training regimes seldom yield any positive results. It is therefore important to identify the most pressing needs at hand and then develop training regimes to address these.

If there is a particular weakness which was addressed in the previous routine but failed to produce any positive results, it means the message was not conveyed in the right manner. Hence the need to find newer and more effective ways of communicating information becomes essential. For the training and development efforts to yield positive results, it first needs to be ensured that the training routine has been carried out appropriately. Careful planning and execution will eventually help improve employee morale and equip them with knowledge that they can put to use to enhance their productivity levels.

About 19% of the employees feel that if they are able to receive more feedback from their employers, they will be able to improve their performance significantly. This is equivalent to higher employee engagement which has the capacity to boost company productivity by about 202%.

## *Reason #7 - They Take On Responsibilities*

When employees are taken into confidence and are able to communicate their concerns with the senior management, they feel valued in the eyes of the employer. This can go a long way in the development process. When they are given their due share of respect and care, the employees feel more inclined to assume bigger responsibilities at the workplace. They feel involved and hence more likely to progress up the hierarchical ladder instead of switching over to another organization. As they begin taking on newer responsibilities, it eventually benefits the organization.

*Some of the most notorious employee relations and disciplinary action cases I have worked with involve employees goofing off on the job, the famous "it's not my job" answer, employees and supervisors having different views of how the job should be completed, and the list goes on. What's even more surprising is when the manager or supervisor start dictating their expectations without asking "Why" and trying to understand the real reason that triggers those behaviors.*

*Take the case of some IT department for example; consider the company is in need of an updated central management system. Generally, the company's own IT department becomes sidelined during this phase. They feel disowned and unvalued which is why they resort to take a back seat while the transition is in place.*

*Moreover, at times, the employees may feel a certain sense of happiness every time the new installation experiences a problem and needs time to be set back up. Quite evidently, the organization is going through a tumultuous phase with no real support from their IT department. The right way to go about this transition is to take the company's IT department in full confidence about the switchover and then conduct the process under their supervision. This way they will feel involved with the whole transition and therefore more likely to participate productively in the process.*

*More so, if the new software poses problems, the IT department will be more likely to spend extra time to fix the problems on their own and to reduce the lag time to a bare minimum. They will assume greater responsibilities to make sure the organization keeps running smoothly and steadily towards its objectives. Consequently, greater employee engagement can be guaranteed.*

The phenomenon stays applicable not just with transitions but also with training for new technological usage. In most cases, acquisition of new software is not as essential as it seems. It has been regarded as one of the worst decisions taken by companies without the involvement of their IT professionals. Consequently, it ends up becoming a major cost center for the company with little or no support from the existing IT experts in the organizations. They are twice as likely to switchover due to employee disengagement.

In a nutshell, employees need recognition and appreciation to keep on working hard for organizational objectives. Salaries, though a major motivational factor, become insignificant after sometime when and if the employer continually denies granting his/her employees with this basic right. As a result, job positions with awesome salary packages but nothing else on offer experience high turnover as compared with other slowly-progressing job roles.

If the appreciation and recognition is adequately backed with learning and development efforts, the results achieved become phenomenal. Not only are the employees sufficiently equipped with knowledge and resources to perform well but also have the right level of motivation which keeps pushing them forward towards their business goals. Resultantly, they can prove to be the major driving force for a significant positive change in the organization. Employees will feel determined to outperform their previous performance scores and achieve newer heights in terms of quality and quantity of work delivered. The apparent increase in their performance indicators will serve as a motivational force for them to keep working harder and achieve greater goals. As they see their scores improve, they will experience a certain sense of achievement—an intrinsic motivational factor.

About 31% of the employees attribute their unproductive time to unclear and ambiguous priorities without direction. So they are unaware about what they need to be doing to achieve what goals. 32% employees believe their unproductive periods can be attributed with ineffective communication channels and supervision which confuses the employees about their objectives and goals.

Lastly, 29% employees believe procrastination is the reason for colossal amounts of wasted hours. The management delays feedbacks which then delays their reaction time and eventually leads to unproductive time periods. In a similar manner, the employees are not awarded their required resources readily which is why their productivity declines.

Learning and development efforts make sure these loopholes are adequately addressed—provided these are being conducted in the right manner. When the employees are taken into confidence about their training goals and business objectives, it automatically informs them about what is expected of them and what they need to do in order to play their role in the organizational development. With a clear focus and direction, the employees are more likely to be able to reach their goals as compared with the previous case. Employers need to identify ways to recognize and appreciate their employees in order to motivate them towards work and strategic goals. Statistically, it's been highlighted that about 69% of the employees believed they would work harder if their organizations have a better recognition and appreciation structure. This means the company has a potential to double their performance if only they can motivate their employees adequately.

Productivity can be quantified in numbers. However, their impact can be felt across the organization. So, if employers are looking for better-looking records and financial statements, they should begin by investing in their workforce and providing them adequate opportunities for development and growth which can help them meet and surpass their targets.

## The notion of improved quality

5S and lean manufacturing training alone do not improve quality; people do. They take pride in doing so by understanding the value behind producing a quality product, and actually care (engage) enough to do it. Some production and training managers can disagree with this, but the truth of the matter is, if your line managers are trained in this process once a year (sometimes less), your supervisors can barely remember 2 of the 5S by the time the training is over. Your line employees who are driving every day production and quality can care less what they stand for, more less applying them. Hence, there is no value to your business in focusing on such training over engaging your team. This does not only improve the productivity quantitatively but also qualitatively. So the company does not only benefit in numbers but also in intangible characteristics of the offering. This eventually plays a role in encouraging customer loyalty.

Most businesses now understand the importance of customer services and quality in their work environment. Customers are willing to pay an extra given their demands for quality services provision are met. Moreover, customers will find reasons to purchase their goods from a particular service provider if only they cherish the relationship with them.

Employers are therefore stressing on quality of work to achieve greater ends. A simple way to achieve this is through learning and development and through employee engagement. Employees feel determined to work harder and steadier if they are satisfied with their jobs; the quality as well as quantity of their produce increases. In the end, employers have a lot to gain from this kind of employee reaction. Equip the employees with the essential resources and the employers will immediately observe a significant improvement in terms of their productivity and dedication towards work. This ensures they have the means to achieve their targets and will therefore be motivated to do so. So the quality of their work also tends to improve.

On-job training, when well-planned and administered correctly, helps improve employee morale. This, in turn, impacts productivity, absenteeism, employee conflicts, and employee turnover positively. Employees feel renewed fervor in working for the company and getting acknowledged for all the hard work they put in. They feel determined to give in their best. Eventually, the quality of their offerings is a hundred times better in all aspects.

In most cases, low employee morale is attached with unchallenging work environment and tasks, negligible or outright no opportunities for growth and development, lack of trust within the hierarchical structure of the organization, lack of or miscommunication of goals and targets, lack of motivation and motivational factors, inflexible working conditions, and lack of autonomy. This is why employee productivity takes a dip before the employee finally decides to switchover to other jobs.

On-job training is believed to increase employee productivity by 40% and employee morale by 35%. This translates into an increased quality of work. Eventually, company's profitability and competitiveness will also improve. However, just as any other development initiative, before launching such program, I urge you to designate who will be accountable for its success. Way too often I observe organizations who claim to train on the job, but have nothing more than a sink or swim system in place, with no guidance and established accountability for success.

## Outperforming Targets

At the commencement of each term, the employees are or should be given a certain set of business targets that they are required to meet. The idea is to ensure the organization is continually moving forward towards progress and development. The company needs to maintain a certain level of profitability in order to be able to pay the employee salaries. Setting targets is not enough on behalf of the employers and managers; they need to show the employees a way to achieve their goals as well. This is because initially the goals may seem too big to achieve. This is done on purpose to ensure the employees have something to push them a step forward from their comfort zone. However, if the employees are not shown a definitive path to achieve these seemingly insurmountable goals, they will become discouraged and might not even try to meet the targets.

The scenario becomes very different when it comes to development. Often, such efforts are focused to overcome imminent weaknesses. It equips the employees with an advanced set of skills that they can use to achieve greater goals. This means the employees are adequately skilled to not only achieve the designated targets but also exceed these. The improvement in key performance indicators makes sure that the employees are motivated to keep progressing. It works both ways—the employees work to improve their scores and the scores keep them motivated to improve further. The businesses can actually benefit greatly from this chain reaction given they are able to provide the right level of commitment, support and involvement.

As the employees learn newer and better ways to perform their duties and to improve their productivity levels, they feel inclined to put it into practice. This clearly depicts a company's dedication towards its employees. In fact, it is seen as an effort to help employees meet their targets. Subsequently, employees reciprocate these efforts by actually working hard and surpassing strategic goals. If correctly aligned with the business objectives, this means the employees will be working together to benefit the business.

It is the general human psyche—people like being challenged. At the same time, they like being challenged about things that are achievable. Setting targets combined with appropriate training and development efforts makes intelligent use of this human behavior to direct positive results. In the end, companies have a lot to benefit if they follow an appropriate course of action.

## *Better Customer Relations*

All business concerns these days are backed by customer relations. No business can survive if it is not being accepted by an appreciable customer base. It is one of the fundamental aspects of running a business—without customers, there is no future. Moreover, achieving one-time sales is not really the motive for most businesses. They need the customers to come in again in order to continue with their business interests. Moreover, they need their existing consumers to pull in more customers through positive word of mouth. The more number of customers a business has over a period of time; it translates into better credibility and profitability.

Better customer relations automatically translate into higher business profitability. This is because better customer relations signify customer satisfaction. In effect, satisfied customers are more likely to indulge in positive business marketing than dissatisfied ones. On the contrary, the latter have the capacity to turn away prospective customers by sharing their bad experiences. Consequently, new customer will avoid interacting with the business in the hope of avoiding frustration and conflict. One of the key factors governing the result of customer relations depends on the quality of produce. Admittedly, a lot of this association depends on how the business treats its customers, interacts with them, and resolves their grievances. But if the customer has no use for the company's offerings or is dissatisfied with its quality, s/he is less likely to indulge in a business transaction with it.

Needless to say that the quality of offering and level of customer relations put forth by customer services representatives both depend on company employees. If they are willing to make a positive change in the organization, it will automatically impact how customers look upon the business. It is therefore in the best interests for all executives to indulge in relative development efforts, relative to their business that do not only keep the employees happy but also instill dedication and hard work on their behalf.

At the other end of the line, the customers' interests are at stake. If they are not adequately protected, it will eventually lead to hefty losses for the company. As the experts say, "The customer is always right!" Prove them wrong and the business is already headed for a steady downfall!

The ability to relate with customers can also be taught to the customer services representatives through appropriate learning and development programs. Such programs do not only teach the representatives how to address and communicate with the customers but also tell them the tips and tricks of developing a long-term relationship with the customers in an instant. The key is to make the customers feel special. If the employees know how to do that, they can eventually win over thousands of customers in favor of the business.

## Overcoming Organizational Weaknesses

Regardless of the efforts made by organization to retain their employees, there are still a few that will leave. Their reason may be progress-oriented, familial or any other for that matter. This creates a vacancy within the organizational hierarchy that needs to be filled quickly in order to maintain their level of productivity. Once their notice period has expired, the company should be able to present the subordinates with a new face and competitive skills in order to keep them motivated towards progress.

Typically, hiring new employees is a tedious task. Not only does it demand a significant portion of business resources in order to reach out, attract, and collect the pool of resumes, an equally extensive time is required to sift through these applications in order to single out the most eligible candidate for the job. The series of tests, interviews and other modes of selection employed by businesses are usually essential in order to identify the right applicant for critical job positions.

Being able to hire new employees at the right time and having the right candidates fill in key job positions is a feat very few organizations excel at. In most cases, the job position stays vacant for a long time after the last occupant has left—at times for months at a stretch! This does not only incur the cost of hiring employees but also that of productivity losses during the vacant period.

Even if this is not the case, employees need to go through adequate training and development programs in order to take the organization forward. Through development initiatives, employees get the chance to identify their weaknesses, work towards improving these areas and also fill in the gaps in the organization that have been made as a result of these weaknesses. As a result, the organization is able to achieve a higher level of competitiveness and hence benefit immensely.

Hiring employees from within the organization for managerial roles is not uncommon. While this minimizes the acclimatization efforts needed to educate the new employee about the organizational culture; I urge leaders to plan early for such changes, and take charge of their succession planning program. Promoting someone simply because they have been in a department for 20 years- no one else is prepared- but yet has not been developed for that position, can only hinder your business. However, with proper planning this can help with positions not remain vacant for long—the job is filled in for at the earliest.

Admittedly, limitation posed by individual expertise does play a role in restricting the benefits put forth by this scheme. For instance, an IT professional cannot perform the tasks and duties of an HR executive or a Marketing expert. No amount of training can help employees achieve this kind of multi-tasking or flexibility. There will always be some intricacies of individual fields of expertise that is best left to the experts. However, vertical movement within the organization is made possible through development efforts. Such measures strengthen the internal organizational infrastructure and hence give the organization a competitive advantage over other companies in the same industry. The organization is built on the foundation of healthy, stable and skilled employees. Given the organization takes care of employees' intrinsic needs in the form of consistent progress and development, it is possible to mend all the missing links for a well-knit and progressive organization.

## Taking the Company to New Heights

When it comes to overcoming weaknesses, the scope cannot be limited to the fact that the company is ready for employee turnover at all times. This also means that the company has the chance to improve its internal structures in order to capitalize on opportunities present in the market. For instance, technological advancements come about with massive improvements in business processes. The idea is to promote automation in order to improve productivity and hence reduce the workload on people. There are innumerable technological innovations made each year out of which quite a few are actually practical for business use. The product is available in the market, so will organizations grab this opportunity to improve their scores?

More often, it takes a long time for organizations to build their confidence in such technological products for a simple reason—they are fads. As fast as they become common in business, they also become obsolete with the same pace. The result is therefore, a massive loss on training investment. On the other hand, inability to do so can put companies at a disadvantage as others grab the opportunity and transform it into millions.

It is therefore important to evaluate the pros and cons of different technological programs carefully before picking a course most appropriate for the organization. The right people (IT professionals in this case) should be taken into confidence in order to multiply the returns. If the company makes the right decision, the training and development efforts can play a pivotal role in maintaining the company's competitiveness and also in providing a tough time to its competitors. As technology progresses, the traditional resources become obsolete for their ineffectiveness and inefficiency. Strategic use of advanced technological products can further business objectives.

## *Long Term Focus Instead of Short Term*

In an attempt to meet targets and business goals, most organizations focus almost extensively on short term achievements while overlooking the long term consequences of their decisions. So while they are able to meet their immediate goals, they are less likely to survive through the years in the same way. A business goal should never be short-term just as a manager should never be short-sighted. The long term implications should be taken into account just as the short term decisions are. This means the business is adequately prepared to take on the challenges put forth through the years.

Employee Development initiatives should be no different, and are to be designed to cover up their immediate problems as well as prepare for future problems, if any. Their focus is multi-dimensional and comprehensive. So businesses can truly prosper in the right sense.

## *Preparing Contingencies for Future*

Considering the fact that human resource is quite unpredictable. Extremely promising performers can leave their organizations in order to pursue bigger goals. At the same time, competitors can become successful in picking out a gem from businesses that can truly put the organizational dynamics at risk. Having others that are prepared to play bigger roles in the organization is what the company needs in order to be fully prepared for these situations at all times.

It prepares contingencies for future. Generally, since too frequent job hopping is not considered likeable on the curriculum vitae, employees are likely to stick around with their jobs for a period of 6 months to 1 year at least even if they absolutely detest their job description. The theory stays valid for people employed at all hierarchical levels. Proper learning and development programs help in retaining employees. It prepares employees to progress through the organizational hierarchy and to assume greater roles within the organization. So when and if the employee leaves, another one is prepared to perform the duties and tasks attributed to the job position. Generally, hiring people to "smaller" job positions is easier than finding the right candidate for high-level jobs.

## *Overcoming Forthcoming Gaps*

Consider this case for an example; for years, a small-sized company has been struggling with its public relations. Since the company does not have inexhaustible resources, there is no separate PR department to take care of the company's dealings outside the office boundaries. The marketing department of the company has been juggling this responsibility along with dozen others that are integral for the business.

The company has expanded considerably through the years with impressive reputation in the market place. People know the company and at times are trying to get in touch with the officials but it is simply not possible to get a contact. It is creating distrust, anxiety and general lack of credibility. The company finally realizes it is short on dedicated PR professionals.

One way to go about it is to place an advertisement and hire someone with prior experience of public relations but no knowledge about the company whatsoever. A better way would be to train the employee who had been taking care of public relation duties in the past and groom him/her into the company's voice.

If the company had been proactive in decision making, it would begin developing a PR specialist in-house long before the realization dawned forcefully on them. As soon as the company starts expanding, it could invest in an employee in the marketing department to take care of this task. Subsequently, a separate department could be created with a unified goal. This means the company is not only enriching the employees' roles within the organization but also that they are proactively preparing for forthcoming gaps in the organizational structure.

### *Lower Costs of Human Resource Management*

Human resource management is one of the most crucial aspects of any business. It is a tricky task to ensure the staffing requirements are fulfilled at all times to reduce productivity losses. One can never truly predict when and if an employee is going to leave—for any reason. Whether it is about employee retention or employee recruitment, the human resource management is entrusted with the responsibility of handling all affairs pertaining to the employees.

## Overcoming the cost of Organizational Parasites

Statistical analysis have shown, about 77% of the businesses are likely to hire new employees in the coming years. About 20% of these are likely to be what I like to call organizational parasites, often referred to as "bad hires". Bad hires are those people that are likely to cost the company more than the benefit they provide for it. For instance, an area of the selection process that is often overlooked but very important is linking employee strength with organizational objectives. There has to be a connection between what they are good at and what your business needs to succeed. If your business needs someone to drive workplace development, find an expert to do just that, not a Human Resources Generalist. Anything outside of that can only constitutes a bad hire which all contributes to high turnover, and impact business profitability.

Employee theft is very common. In 2008, the loss caused to businesses as a result of employee theft was estimated to be about $15.9 billion! About 30% entrepreneurial ventures meet their unfortunate demise due to employee theft. On the same note, about 75% of the employees are likely to steal from their employers at some point or the other. Bad hires simply magnify the probability of businesses falling into this trap. An employee who steals and then gets away with it serves as a source of motivation for other employees to steal too. This chain goes on till the employees end up stealing so much that the company no longer has enough resources to survive. Therefore, the company faces bankruptcy and eventually closes down.

Workplace homicide is also emerging as one of the major concerns for most human resource professionals. Violence at the work place does not only tarnish the reputation of the company but also gives rise to security issues. According to an estimate, about 13% of all workplace accidents and fatalities are attributed to workplace violence. Most businesses are likely to encounter at least one such case in their organization at some point or the other.

Another way employees end up costing their employers more than the benefit they offer is through fraudulent claims. At times, employees try to manipulate the results of workers' compensation in order to yield more benefit. A small injury may be exaggerated and presented as a major one, an old injury might be posed to be a new one and at times, even non-existing injuries would be claimed for. This can cost the company significantly in terms of compensation premiums, etc.

And then there are the fraudulent claims made by employees towards their employers based on racial discrimination, sexual assaults, and other similar workplace demeanors. Thousands of claims are filed each year by employees. In 79% of the cases, the employer loses the verdict and ends up paying a rather hefty sum in compensation. This further deteriorates the case.

This means the cost of a bad hire can cost employers anywhere between $25,000 and $4 million! In most cases, the company is obliged to pay a compensation of no less than $1 million! This adequately highlights the importance of thorough research and screening efforts made while selecting the candidates from the pool of applicants. If the recruiter falls prey to a bad hire, it may put the company's survival on the line.

It is not likely the employee would approach the company himself/herself looking for an opportunity to strike. In a standard recruiting process, their curriculum vita comes in through the regular portal of applications possibly alongside a hundred other viable candidates. This means the recruitment process itself has its own procedures and costs other than the cost of a bad hire.

The hiring process begins by placing strategic advertisements across different mediums of communication to attract applicants. This includes writing the advertisement copy complete with job specifications and job descriptions and then publishing it across different portals. This phase can take about 1 hour to 1 and a half hours. The estimated cost can range between $40 and $450 depending on the choice of portals. The first resumes are likely to come in within 200 seconds of job postings. The next step is to go through the applications. This can be quite a tiring process as the recruiters move through all the applications which can number in hundreds! On average, if the applications are being read by a human recruiter, about 5-7 seconds are likely to be spent on each resume. A lucrative resume may receive about 5 minutes of the recruiter's attention. After going through all the CVs, a list of selected candidates is prepared. The time spent on this activity can range between a day and a week depending on the number of applications. Also, the costs begin at about $600.

Alternatively, the resumes can be put through the application tracking system but to great disadvantage. For instance, some extremely promising candidates may be rejected simply based on the lack of key words usage. Likewise, some "bad hires" may occur due to lack of qualification but better structure of the CVs. There is no realistic estimate about how much time this phase can take but it is likely to cost thousands of dollars in monthly subscriptions of such programs, the need for technical resource to manage these systems and the cost of surfing through the applications pool.

The next phase for some positions includes scheduling tests, video conferences, and/or other mediums of preliminary evaluation before getting into a face-to-face interaction and also communicating the dates, times and venues to the applicants. At times, the process can take more than one week to execute completely. The phone bills added with the cost of materials can cost more than $100.

The interviews are then scheduled for the finest few shortlisted after the preliminary evaluation. This includes the cost of hiring interviewers, phone calls to inform the relevant candidates about their schedules and other miscellaneous expenses made along the way. The cost may be around $50 and the time may range between 1 day and 1 week.

The materials used during the interview (if any) are another expense incurred for recruitment. These expenses can range between $75 and $1000 or even more! Lastly, once the most probably candidate is identified, the wrapping up procedure may take another day or two in which the contracts are laid out, negotiated and then signed, the prep talk and orientation is given and the employee is told when to start with his/her job. The cost can range up to $200!

The procedure is quite lengthy. In some cases, the job position may remain vacant for a period of 45 to 95 days at a stretch. This further adds to the cost of hiring in terms of productivity losses. The aforementioned estimate does not include a realistic figure to point towards the time and cost required for training the new recruit in order for him/her to be able to perform the desired duties. Furthermore, even after going through the process, the organization may still end up with a parasite, incurring lethal losses!

Needless to say, the hiring process is quite complex and full of uncertainties. It is not easy for companies to find replacement for their current employees. On top of this, there is always a chance the company may end up making a "bad hire". Thus employee development and retention is the key to reducing hiring costs.

Investing a small portion of this amount on employee development initiatives can do the trick. When employees perceive consistent improvement in them as well as in the organization they are working in, they are less inclined to leave. As a result, employers can save millions on hiring costs. In another estimate, it was noted that an employee which leaves incurs almost triple the amount of his/her salary in losses for the company. Admittedly, this does not mean the turnover ratio can be reduced to zero. Employees may leave for reasons other than organizational weaknesses. In such cases, internal recruitment might be a better alternative to fill in the job position.

## Alternatives to Salary Raises

Adequate emphasis has been placed on the fact that learning and development opportunities are considered more motivational for employees as compared with salary packages. Not only this, the former almost plays an important role in increasing employee retention, improving the company's productivity, improving the organizational culture and improving the "human" aspect of business transactions.

However, if evaluated through another perspective, it is also an undeniable fact that about 22% of employee turnover is attributed to salary inadequacy. If the employees do not have enough resources to provide for their basic needs, they will most definitely try to overcome this barrier before looking at career advancement or development opportunities. Market compatible pay packages are therefore an essential aspect of remuneration and employee retention. If employees feel undervalued or under-compensated, they will most likely jump ship when the first lucrative opportunity is presented to them.

However, there are other non-monetary benefits that can go a long way in keeping employees engaged and happy. They need not only be compensated in monetary terms in order to make them feel valued. Here are some of the other forms of compensation that are known to yield higher job satisfaction and involvement comparable to higher salaries. Many organizations across a wide spectrum are already using these techniques for greater gains.

## *Mystery Surprises*

Everyone likes surprises provided they are good. As an employer, you can build a special box/carton with a number of special benefits stated on them. Each day, the employees will pick one ticket out of the box and enjoy the special privilege written on it. For instance, some people can get a few extra minutes during the break time, a voucher for a meal at a good restaurant, a day to act as another employee in the organization, a job swap with someone in another department and so on and so forth. Keep the surprises small but real. The employee morale will improve significantly just as their attendance scores would. Who would want to miss out on a surprise?!

## *Flexible Schedules*

This technique normally works wonders with top performers who cannot be rewarded in monetary form, they can still be rewarded with other benefits such as flexible schedules. This can be in the form of certain days that are shorter than others, the flexibility to work from home on a few days, a special leverage during the summer months, or anything similar to this. Being top performers, the likelihood of them working equitably to other employees will be high. Nevertheless, they can enjoy a special privilege and motivate others to outperform their goals and do the same.

## *Free Tickets to Events*

Most people like their social lives. But if they see their employers contributing positively towards it, the emotion is well-received. In all parts of the world, innumerable events are held each year belonging to different genres. For instance, the sporting games, the musical performances, the concerts, the movie screenings, the live stage performances, and so on and so forth.

Employers can hand out a few free tickets to their employees in areas of their interest in order to encourage their social interactions. Employers can also set in a budget—a designated number of free passes per month or per year. When the employee is giving in at least so much of his/her time to work, he/she does deserve a break. What is more, since the company will be approaching the event managers for tickets, it is possible for the company to get amazing discounts on the bulk purchase. So this means free tickets will not only make the employees happy but also cost less!

## *Internet Promotion*

Most employees like writing their names in search engines and searching for their social mentions across the internet. The first few results are likely to be the person's own social profiles. But there is nothing like a mention on the company's official website properly keyed to emerge in the search results.

Companies can try building their employees profiles on their official websites or at least post about the top performer of the week/month on their official web pages (their own website as well as on other social media websites). So when the employee searches for his/her name, they see much more valuable results than simply their social profiles. They can also brag about their achievements in association with the company which will eventually reinforce the company's foothold.

## *Certificates of Appreciation*

Certificates of appreciation are an old method of appreciation yet they still work just as well. Companies can use certificates of appreciation in order to recognize, applaud and commend a job that is well done! It adds credibility to the employee's professional profile and is therefore considered as a good notion on behalf of the company. Moreover, employees like to frame the certificate and hang it in their cubicles in the office place in order to flaunt their achievements and also to stay motivated towards a central cause. While the certificates almost cost nothing for the company to print and present, the intangible benefits achieved from such an exchange are truly remarkable.

## *Educational Support*

Education is fundamental for progress in order to climb the corporate ladder these days. People are realizing the importance of education and therefore grabbing every opportunity to advance themselves as far as their academic career is concerned. Companies can further reinforce this behavior by providing educational support in the form of scholarships, flexible schedules, partial contributions etc. This clearly shows the company's interest in employee grooming and is therefore looked upon as a positive notion. In fact, this is seen as a bigger motivational factor as compared with salary raises. Nevertheless, it can have a profound impact on the employee's perception towards the company.

## *Title changes*

Promotions need not always be coupled with a fancy increase in salaries. Awarding the employee with another job title also plays an important role in keeping him/her motivated towards the job. The job title is the one thing which says a lot about what the person does at the job without really exposing everything. A job title that reads "assistant manager" or "executive manager" is infinitely better than one which says "trainee" or "intern". So if a company cannot grant their employees with an impressive pay rise, the least that can be done is to increase the job title in value which compensates for the pay.

However, one thing needs to be kept in mind. A promotion of any sort is almost always linked with an increase in the salary package in the mind of the employee. So if an employer is planning to offer the former half of the package alone, it needs to be communicated in an intelligent manner so that the employee does not feel let down.

If the company concerns over why a salary increase is not viable are shared with the employee, it will help him/her feel valued and integral to the equation. Communicate the ideas well and in advance so heartbreaks can be minimized.

## *Bonuses*

The key to keeping employees motivated is to provide them adequate recognition for their efforts. It may be in non-monetary forms or monetary forms. As long as the employees feel valued, they will be motivated to upkeep the good performance and also encourage other employees to do the same.

If salary raises are not a viable option, employers can go for one-time cash bonuses that are impressive and lucrative. If even this is not viable, employers can alternatively go for sponsoring employee travel plans. For instance, granting a company sponsored holiday in the employee's choice of destination or sponsoring certain benefits along the way—like a yacht trip etc. There are many things an employer can do to truly compensate the employee for his/her work. Where there is a will, there is a way.

The last few paragraphs effectively summarize some ideas how employers can compensate their employees other than salary increments. The key is recognition, appreciation, and motivation. Build an ongoing communication and coaching relationship with the people you manage and hold them accountable to do the same with their subordinates. This will help in understanding them better and which reward is more appreciated by each one which plays a major role in motivation.

*In one of the employee appreciation efforts I supported, was about a week long where the company sponsored lunch every day of the week, gave out gift cards and different prizes, lot of hefty stuff throughout the day. We thought everything was perfect until the feedback came in. When asked what could be done differently, 65% of the employees admitted that they would have preferred ½ a day off during that week in lieu of the gift cards and monetary prizes.*

*Lessons learned from the results: Were that we could have done a better job at understanding the demographics of that particular organization and identifying the ideal rewards for motivation.*

In essence, any technique that achieves these purposes is likely to yield positive results for the company. There are lots of other avenues an employer can take to motivate employees. If the leaders can look closely at their workforce and determine the factors that encourage the employees to perform and attain greater goals, it will help the company prosper beyond the conventional realms.

# EMPLOYEE DEVELOPMENT AND ITS IMPACT ON ORGANIZATIONS

Several companies have indulged in training and development efforts for their employees with distinctive results. It is a well-proven fact that training and development yields positive results in many ways. However, it largely depends on how well the routine is carried out. If the employees feel sidelined or "pushed around", they are less likely to respond productively.

Education and development efforts need to be orchestrated in an intelligent manner. I use the term education over training because the intended purposes are different. When an employer takes on the stand to educate its workforce, regardless of the topics, it creates more of a commitment to the issue at hand from their part, than merely conducting a training session and forgetting about the subject later. The employees should feel involved and enticed by the program instead of being bored with words. Multiple tools are available for this process which can be tailored to the group in question and later reinforced with on-the-job coaching to keep the interest intact. As adult learners, employees need to understand (through education) and see direct value to their job when new principles are taught, whatever employees learn willingly will be retained in their memories for twice as long as otherwise.

At the same time, it is important to keep in mind that development efforts are never really inexpensive. It has been estimated that instructor-led training programs take about 43 hours to prepare and can cost up to $5,934 per training session. In contrast with this, e-learning programs can take anywhere between 79 hours and 490 hours of preparation according to their complexity levels. Consequently, their costs range between $10,054 and $50,371. Needless to say, these efforts need to be well planned and well executed in order to reap impressive returns on this investment!

On average, organizations are known to have a training budget of $145.5 million annually. This amount is roughly 4.52% of the company's payroll expenses. Broadly stated, the company resources are not sufficient enough to indulge in training efforts repeatedly. The training hours are also considered in productivity losses as this is the time period when most of the employees are not technically working but rather preparing for future needs. Hence the training efforts need to be planned and implemented after significant thought to minimize all kinds of losses to a bare minimum and to increase the return on investment significantly.

Unless a leadership team is committed to advocate education over simple routine training, development will not flourish. Education and learning is ongoing, and has to be tackled early on in the development process. I always advise against those impulsive hour long/days or even weeks of training sessions for subordinates on needs that are normally not assessed correctly, that no one is accountable to reinforce in the workplace, or employees simply don't see a need for in relation to meeting business objectives.

Here are a couple of case studies to help you understand how development impacts businesses all around the world. This also intends to highlight the essential elements of development which ensure success and long term retention of these programs.

## _Siemens's Training and Development Efforts_

Siemens is also known for incorporating another important organizational change to promote managerial bonding. They introduced the culture of singing in choir to promote interdepartmental bonding. The senior management was taught and rehearsed to sing in choir for their employees and to boost their morale while doing so. In fact, the choir was selected to perform at all major informal company meetings like the Christmas gatherings.

It was initially believed to be an insurmountable task but was eventually integrated well into the organization. Not only was the senior management able to learn and adapt to the challenge readily but also they used the same technique to bond with their subordinates in an informal setting. The method has been adopted by other trainers as well. The method was so effective that it eventually won recognition and the Prudential People Development award from the Arts and Business Awards in 2010. Since then, the technique came to be used by other participants in the training industry as well.

## Siemens Graduate Programs

Siemens is never short of development efforts to ensure continued progress. They launched their graduate programs in the year 2005 to help students build specialization in their desired fields. The "institute" is divided into three broad segments—engineering, information technology and business. All employees are allowed to discuss and select the specialization of their interest. Contrary to popular belief, the courses are not thrust upon the employees but rather suggested by the managers through mutual consent and discussion.

The employees are exposed to numerous challenges most companies face on a daily basis and they are allowed to put their problem-solving skills to practice. It is a form of on-job training which helps employees understand the company's working and also to gain hands on experience. The students shuffle between their jobs and the four year graduation program while learning about the realities of life in a way that prepares them for all challenges of life.

Not only this, Siemens as a company also supports on-going educational programs for their employees. They can continue to pursue their academic careers while on their jobs so that they can remain abreast with the latest from their respective fields. This eventually prepares them to perform their roles within the organization in a better manner and sustain a higher degree of competitiveness in the market place.

As a matter of fact, this form of training and development effort on behalf of companies has remained quite popular. Employees consider it as a plus point if their companies are willing to support them through their academic endeavors. Such employees sustain higher levels of job satisfaction and are therefore twice more likely to remain with their current employer for more than one year at a stretch.

## _The Learning Campus_

It is another one of Siemens' notable efforts at training and development of their employees. The Learning Campus has remained exceptionally popular between masses and the employees of Siemens have extremely high hopes for the program. According to their official resources, there are over 26 core learning programs currently being executed at their Learning Campus with over 4,068 employees from 70 countries enrolled in them. The Core Learning Programs at this Siemens institute facility are formulated after in-depth analysis of ongoing business needs. This means the company is actively participating in bridging the gap in employee potential.

The employees also look upon these programs as a vital tool to improve their performances within the organization. The Learning Campus works closely with individual business units in developing and designing the structure of different training programs. They aim to build identified core competencies in employees and achieve these results in a guaranteed way.

The reason why the Learning Campus has been popular and successful in the past is because the programs are developed by the people for the people with mutual understanding. The program has made a positive change in the lives of over 4,000 employees in Siemens and continues to do the same for more people year after year.

## Aldi's Development Efforts

Aldi is a Germany-based global chain of discounted supermarket stores that has established presence in the United States, the United Kingdom, and several other countries across the world. It is known to have established its presence at over 9,600 locations. This phenomenal amount of business expansion can largely be attributed with its training and development efforts.

Aldi's main center of focus is on offering good quality products at lowest possible prices to relieve its customers from the burden of financial depression. It carefully selects the suppliers from which the goods are to be purchased and ensures the most competitive deals are drawn. The supplies are purchased in bulk to receive the maximum discounts. The savings reaped as a result of such measures are passed on to the customers who enjoy unparalleled savings on their favorite products.

Aldi recognizes and places special emphasis on training and development programs for its employees. It understands that in order to remain competitive in the business environment, it is important to invest and develop employees in the right direction. Coupled with talent management programs and strategic human resource planning, the company is able to maintain its competitiveness even in economically adverse times.

Aldi predicts its current human resource availability and the future needs in this regard as and when it decides to inaugurate another location. It plans not only for the number of workers that will be needed to take care of the new facility but also plans for the skill sets required by these individuals to tackle the challenges posed by the new settlement. The company then indulges in recruiting employees for different roles and also puts them through elaborate training and development programs to ensure they have the desired competencies to be able to manage their roles in the organization effectively.

Given the pace of their business expansion, it is quite evident that their current human resource availability is incapable of meeting up with the business needs of tomorrow. This helps the company respond proactively to this employee gap. They do not only indulge in the best industry practices with respect to recruitment but also offer the best salary packages that are well received by the applicants.

For each job position that it advertises, a detailed and well-rounded job description is laid out to ensure the company as well as the applicants are on the same page while exchanging the applications. Continued employee development is another reason behind their phenomenal success.

The company invests in training and development programs at all levels. During the first year, employees are given a basic wholesome training routine which informs them about the working of the retail business as well as the individual stores, regional tasks, logistics concerns, financial planning, and trading transactions. The employees are given the basic comprehensive understanding of the whole process while also being trained to look after the different functions within the organization to make sure the business objectives are being met from the first day at work.

Aldi particularly invests in on-job training for numerous benefits. For instance, on job training reduces the loss of work hours and ensures the company's productivity remains unhampered. It commonly uses on-job coaching from superiors, mentoring, job rotation, and observational training to ensure the employees are able to learn those skills that are required by their jobs. Not only this, but this also ensures the employees are able to put these skills into practice as they remain under constant supervision of store managers/trainers.

The business also offers apprenticeship programs. It helps the younger recruits achieve productive results from their life and learning. For instance, employees entering Aldi's apprenticeship programs usually begin at the age of 16 to 18 years. With time, these employees undergo vigorous on-job and off-job training routines that help them progress through the organizational hierarchy readily. Within a period of years, these apprentices become eligible to assume the role of store managers and other core managerial job positions! It is therefore considered rather lucrative for most students.

These are just two examples from the corporate world. There are plenty of other examples that have used employee development and training programs strategically to meet business objectives. When aligned properly with well-defined business goals, training and development efforts can not only be used to bridge the gaps in employee potential but also prepare proactively for the challenges likely to be faced by the organization in near future. Development therefore, does not only ensure business competitiveness, but also its survival.

The size of the organization does not affect its capacity to indulge in or make use of strategic training and development programs. The small scaled organizations also have a lot to gain from such efforts both in terms of improved productivity as well as business expansion. That said, it is needless to say employee development is integral to business success. Most top rated businesses have already identified the importance of a good development program for their employees while an increasing number of employers are turning towards this medium to attain competitiveness.

The question then remains: are you ready to make this vital change

CONCLUSION

- - - - - - - - - - - - - - - - - - - - - - - - - - - - - - - - - - - - - - - - - - - - - - - - - - - - - - - - - - - - - - - - - - - - -

It is evident that engaged employees are an important asset to any company. Gallup carried out a research back in 2012 by observing 263 unique studies that covered 49928 business units across 34 countries.

The study focused on how engagement of employees was important in good economic times as well as the bad ones. James K. Harter, Gallup's chief scientist stated:

*"What has been most surprising to me, as a researcher, is the consistency of the findings during very different economic times"*, *"In good economic times, engagement is the difference between good and great. In bad economic times, engagement is the difference between sinking and holding your own."*

There is a strong link between employee development and employee engagement. The former can be used as a means of enhancing the skill and abilities of the company's employees, thus engaging them. So how can all this affect a business's results?

It does so in several ways. Firstly, development and training of employees significantly increases the employee retention rates, which is an imperative for a business in today's cutting-edge industries where competition is at all-time high. Nothing can stunt the growth and success of a business more than losing highly skilled and experienced employees to the competition.

Secondly, employee development enhances the productivity levels by equipping the staff with all the skills that are required to perform their jobs in the best manner possible. It removes bad habits, it encourages them to function effectively by providing them recognition and rewards for their hard work, and it boosts the morale of the overall workforce, particularly when their career growth is directly linked with the growth of the company.

According to the Gallup research, those businesses that had higher rates of engagement (as a result of comprehensive training and development programs), had extremely low turnover rates, had low rates of absenteeism, employee theft was down to almost nil, safety indicants and accidents were down to all-time low levels. Apart from this, those companies also reported higher numbers of customer loyalty, increased productivity as well as profitability.

An extract from the Gallup report indicated the following improvements occurred as a result of carrying out development and training programs which led to increased employee engagement rates:

- o 37 percent lower absenteeism.
- o 25 percent lower turnover (in high-turnover organizations).
- o 65 percent lower turnover (in low-turnover organizations).
- o 28 percent less shrinkage (employee and/or customer theft).
- o 48 percent fewer employee safety incidents.
- o 41 percent fewer quality incidents or defects.

o 10 percent higher customer loyalty/engagement.
o 21 percent higher productivity.
o 22 percent higher profitability.

Thus, it can be seen that there is a direct link between employee development and the success of businesses. A loyal, happy and engaged workforce contributes to the success of a business, and if the management utilizes these tools to their advantage they thereby can yield the results they desire.

An employee's decision to remain with the current employer is based on a number of intricately linked factors, such as job satisfaction, employee engagement, motivation, training and development opportunities, being valued, being productive, and so on and so forth. However, the least important of these is the compensation plan provided the employees basic needs are being fulfilled conveniently.

In order to engage the employees and prevent costly turnovers, employers need to provide their subordinates with a vision of progress. The employees should be able to see the opportunity for growth and advancement. The system as a whole should be moving towards betterment for the benefit of the employees, the company, the customers and everyone else involved with it. So if companies are trying to improve employee retention, they stand a better chance of achieving this goal by providing the employees with the right focus instead of hefty salaries. The latter can give rise to job dissatisfaction at some point in time or the other. But a growth and development-oriented focus never does so.

In the end, it is up to the employers to decide!

When it's all said and done, what I want organizational leaders to take from this book is that there is great value to be achieved in developing people and arming them with the tools to succeed. Employees are a fundamental aspect of business performance; the sooner this is realized, the better they can make use of their strategic workforce and compete strongly in the market place. It is a change process that has to start at the top; it has to be part of the culture that the organization breathes and lives by.

To your business success.

Sophia Sanchez

## ABOUT THE AUTHOR

Sophia Sanchez is the founder of Develop For Results International, a boutique consulting firm that helps business leaders identify people develop and change management strategies to retain talent, engage their workforce and strategically align talent management with business objectives. DFRI prides itself in providing well-researched proven business solutions through a people development approach. Personally, Sophia has written over 100 articles on performance management, organizational culture, change management, and business growth. She has shared her expertize on talent management with many small and large organizations in the U.S. and abroad.

For information on upcoming titles and projects, please visit DevelopForResults.com

Or email
Sophia.sanchez@DevelopForResults.com

www.ingramcontent.com/pod-product-compliance
Lightning Source LLC
Chambersburg PA
CBHW060610200326
41521CB00007B/720